# Praise for *The New Managerial Mentor*

"The managerial competencies set forth in *The New Managerial Mentor* and the emphasis on co-learning throughout the organization are essential to a company's success over the next decade. The mentoring model not only highlights the changes required of managers; it provides a way for workers at all levels to get the *right* things done and achieve the personal satisfaction of helping to move the organization ahead."

Jo Ann Peeples, Manager, Labor Relations and Training,
Saco Defense, Inc.

"A timely and important book in these turbulent times of change. This is an excellent, highly readable, and enormously useful book for managers. All employees need to think of themselves as lifelong learners, and, more importantly, managers need to become learning leaders to facilitate this process. I highly recommend this book to all managers who want to lead their organizations into the twenty-first century."

Marilyn G. Bechtold, National Board of Certified Counselors,
Director of Career Management, Murro Consulting, Inc.

"I really liked it! Pat Fritts's description of the skill/mind-sets for learning leaders is especially relevant for today's health care environment. I especially liked the inventories and checklists useful for self-analysis and possible training. A good read that brings together much of the current thinking in this area."

Jonathan R. Sheff, MSW/MPH,
President of Resource Management Consultants

"Written for all the managers who think mentoring takes too much time, this book will help you keep your job or get a better one. Filled with tools and insightful self-assessments, it will help you develop your personal mentoring strategy. Should be in every leader's library, dog-eared and highlighted—or better yet, buy two, one for you and one to share with a colleague."

Kelly Pedersen, Career Management Training, SRP

# The New Managerial Mentor

# The New Managerial Mentor

Becoming a
Learning Leader
to Build
Communities
of Purpose

## Patricia J. Fritts

Davies-Black Publishing
Palo Alto, California

Published by Davies-Black Publishing, an imprint of Consulting Psychologists Press, Inc., 3803 East Bayshore Road, Palo Alto, CA 94303; 800-624-1765.

Special discounts on bulk quantities of Davies-Black books are available to corporations, professional associations, and other organizations. For details, contact the Director of Book Sales at Davies-Black Publishing, an imprint of Consulting Psychologists Press, Inc., 3803 East Bayshore Road, Palo Alto, CA 94303; 650-691-9123; Fax 650-988-0673.

Cover photo: Photonica

02 01 00 99 98    10 9 8 7 6 5 4 3 2 1
Printed in the United States of America

**Library of Congress Cataloging-in-Publication Data**
Fritts, Patricia J.
    The new managerial mentor : becoming a learning leader to build communities of purpose / Patricia J. Fritts. — 1st ed.
      p. cm.
    Includes bibliographical references and index.
    ISBN 0-89106-120-7
    1. Leadership. 2. Mentoring. 3 Organizational learning
I. Title.
HF57.7.F755   1998
658.4'092—dc21

98-25919
CIP

FIRST EDITION
First printing 1998

Dedicated to
J. M. S. and B. F. S.

# Contents

CONTENTS

# PREFACE

Mentoring is a controversial topic in current management circles. Although one-on-one mentoring programs have long been part of management development at such major corporations as Avon, Xerox, and General Electric, the emerging concept of the "learning organization" has sparked renewed interest in mentoring. While many organizations are implementing new mentoring programs, some managers remain skeptical about the value of such programs. Managers in downsized organizations, for example, are typically focused on personal survival. They have little time or energy for mentoring and tend to see ambitious younger people as threats. Managerial survivors do not feel comfortable mentoring those they fear may take their jobs away.

One reason for differing views on the value of mentoring is the lack of a common definition of what comprises effective mentoring in times of radical organizational change. Until recently, many mentoring programs were diversity driven to ease the entry of women and minorities into the workplace. Other programs were informal and were intended to provide opportunities for young, high-potential managers, usually white males, to ride to success on the coattails of senior managers.

Now, leading-edge companies are looking at mentoring as a relatively low-cost way to develop flexible, adaptive networks of learners. These comprise the learning organizations—companies committed to the continual development of individuals and groups to meet changing business needs—who see mentoring as a key human resource strategy. Learning organizations use mentoring as a way to ensure that they have the leadership talent they need to move their companies into the twenty-first century.

All of the case studies in the chapters that follow are based on real experiences in the author's consulting practice. To protect client confidentiality, however, names of people and organizations have been changed and all the examples used in the text represent composites of real people and situations.

## The Managerial Survivors

Managers—particularly those who are corporate survivors—represent an excellent pool of potential mentors. Facing an uncertain future, many survivors have reacted to downsizing in dysfunctional ways. According to David Noer (1993), an expert on the psychological effects of downsizing, helping managerial survivors take personal responsibility for learning is the best way to cure what he calls "survivor sickness." Managerial survivors need to be encouraged to see mentoring as a way to engage in new learning by helping others learn.

Research by Heckscher (1995) indicates that, contrary to the common view, most corporate survivors actually maintain their loyalty to the organization. For such loyalists, the old organization was a tightly knit community of people with

deeply shared values. It was the undermining of these com-
munal ties through downsizing that left people adrift and
angry yet mired in a defensive loyalty to the old ways.

According to Heckscher, some companies were able to
effect successful organizational transitions and replace traditional ties with new communities of purpose driven by a common vision of the future of the business. Managers of these
companies were able to take a broader view of their jobs and
were reenergized and optimistic about the future.

Loyalty is a center-stage issue in downsized organizations.
When the informal ties that hold people together are broken,
there is no context for cooperation. Some organizations have
tried to sweep away the past through large-scale reengineering. These initiatives often fail to achieve the desired results
because survivors either passively resist or are unable to
change fast enough. "Bottom-up" attempts to empower survivors have been equally unsuccessful as survivors become
even more anxious and immobilized by the loss of traditional
boundaries.

Effective organizational change is not best achieved by
attempts to sweep away the past. It is better achieved through
the planful implementation of continual learning practices
that integrate the best of the past with a challenging vision of
the future. Experienced managers can act as key integrators
in the learning process and, in so doing, find new meaning in
their work and share in the creation of communities of purpose. In communities of purpose, survivors are not tied to
old loyalties; instead they are united in pursuit of meaningful
goals and the opportunity to engage in collaborative learning.
Corporate communities of purpose achieve what all genuine
communities do: They provide a sound basis for stable and
cooperative relationships.

Just as corporations should not attempt to sweep away the past, managers should not throw out the past in the interest of starting anew. Both personal and organizational transformations are better achieved through a building-block process that incorporates the learning of the past into a vision of the future. The role of the new managerial mentor described in this book provides a viable way for managerial survivors to build on their accumulated knowledge and expertise in ways that will serve both their personal growth needs and the business needs of the organization.

## Becoming a Learning Leader

The concept of mentor as learning leader replaces the old view of mentors as senior managers who personally nurtured favored "sons" and "daughters." Learning leaders are managerial mentors who network across organizational boundaries to address the real-time learning needs of the business. They use their managerial expertise to coordinate projects and make sure that people develop the necessary knowledge and skills to get the job done right.

Learning leaders do not boss people or limit themselves to one-on-one coaching. In fact, they often have limited face-to-face contact with the people they are mentoring and use structured feedback from co-workers of the people being mentored to pinpoint development tasks. Heckscher (1995) likens such mentors to "point people" who are continually on tap as expert resources for project teams across the organization.

Becoming a learning leader is an excellent way for managers to develop a broader perspective and capitalize on their knowledge of the organization. Actively committing to becoming a learning leader enables managers to extricate themselves from such dysfunctional behaviors as defensive withdrawal or excessive individualism. Learning leaders integrate both the hard and the soft side of management. With a strong focus on the business, they actively cooperate with other learners to build communities of purpose.

Rejuvenated managers become both independent and interdependent thinkers and doers. With roots in the organization, these managerial mentors can serve as valuable stabilizing forces in times of chaotic change. By transforming themselves into learning leaders, they replace old ties with a fresh sense of shared purpose and direction.

Organizational transformation cannot happen in the absence of collective learning. Managerial mentors must take the lead in promoting continual learning as a way of being. They must reach out to people in the organization and listen, reflect, and engage in dialogue with those who look to them for guidance.

In quoting software executive David Boulton, Aubrey and Cohen (1995) provide an excellent capsule description of the work of the learning leader: "I see the mentor in the richest sense as someone who is dancing around the edges of a human being, extending his or her being, and who at the same time has the wisdom to be a facilitator" (p. 21). This mentoring mission not only enables managers to use their wisdom in the service of others, it provides the mentor with an unparalleled opportunity for personal learning and generativity.

## Cultivating Learning Networks

The learning network is a new organizational form for the Information Age. It is a radical departure from the old bureaucratic and informal mentoring networks. According to

Aubrey and Cohen, the learning network is "one in which members agree to common strategy, goals, principles, methods, and roles for exchanging knowledge, skills, and resources" (p. 28). The learning network represents a shift from the informal to the formal and a new emphasis on learning together in "real-work" settings. The learning network is where managerial mentors do their work.

In their 1994 book on networks, Lipnack and Stamps make the point that because organizations are straddling the industrial and information eras, their structures are usually a combination of hierarchy, teams, and networks. While stressing the advantages of networks, the authors caution that creating a workable form of organization calls for "understanding what teams can do, when hierarchy applies, what is useful in bureaucracy, what circumstances call for networks—and how to fit them all together" (p. 20). Experienced managers, with one foot in the past and the other in the future, can help their organizations create effective transitional structures in changing times.

Reenergized managers help their organizations foster a new form of loyalty based on teamwork, innovative thinking, and the creation of breakthrough products and services for the Information Age. The managerial mentoring role calls for the ability to work effectively with diverse groups and manage complex networks of connections and relationships.

In the Information Age, learning leaders must build strong personal relationships both inside and outside of their organizations. While managing relationships has always been a key factor in managerial success, it will become even more critical in the new era. As hierarchical walls crumble, the new managerial mentors must become active leaders in building cooperative, task-driven relationships across all traditional boundaries.

Managerial mentors will become strategic brokers. Their role in networks will be to help individuals and teams identify problems, access resources, and acquire the requisite knowledge and skills to continually achieve top-level performance. As links to the past and bridges to the future, managerial mentors will have a critical role to play in helping their organizations make a successful transition into the Information Age. In the chapters that follow, you will learn how to become a new managerial mentor.

The book comprises three parts: Part One provides an introduction to the concept of the new managerial mentor and describes how, as learning leaders, managerial mentors can help their organizations move successfully into the twenty-first century. Part Two details the four roles of the new managerial mentor: Collaborator, Innovator, Producer, and Integrator. It presents diverse case studies and assessment tools to help prospective learning leaders identify their development needs in the specific competency areas associated with each of the four mentoring roles. Part Three provides an overview of what the twenty-first century will look like and how managerial mentors can serve others by creating collaborative learning experiences to help build new organizational communities of purpose.

# ACKNOWLEDGMENTS

Special thanks are due to the many colleagues and clients who provided me with the ideas and experiences that led to this book. I am especially grateful to all of the managers and professionals in the diverse organizations I have worked with over the last decade who willingly shared their thoughts and feelings about what it takes to survive and thrive in the turbulent organizations of the '90s.

During the writing of this book, many people offered constant encouragement, advice, and support. I would especially like to thank B. Jeanette Winn, Marita S. Bowden, and Marcia Black for their unflagging confidence in my ability to complete the project, particularly on those occasions when I felt like abandoning the whole endeavor. Finally, I am very grateful to Lee Langhammer Law, who first encouraged me to write the book, and her team of professionals at Davies-Black Publishing who helped bring it to reality.

# ABOUT THE AUTHOR

PATRICIA J. FRITTS, Ed.D., has over thirty years of experience as a corporate human resource executive, organizational consultant, and career transition counselor. She consults with large and small companies, nonprofit organizations, and government agencies to help them meet the challenges of organizational change. With particular expertise in leadership development and work team effectiveness, she also coaches managers on how to become self-directed learners in transitional times.

Dr. Fritts is the author of numerous career management and personal development publications, including a video education program for managers on how to support employees with life-threatening illnesses and a computerized profile for assessing individual and organizational stress factors. A member of the Society for Human Resource Management, the Organization Development Network, and the Greenleaf Center for Servant-Leadership, she holds a doctorate in counseling from Boston University and has served as an adjunct faculty member at universities in Massachusetts, Maine, and Arizona.

PART ONE | **MENTORING IN THE LEARNING ORGANIZATION**

THE FIRST PART OF THE BOOK provides an introduction to a new kind of managerial mentor, called the *learning leader*. Learning leaders, unlike traditional mentors, are active leaders of change. They use their experience and the experience of others to participate in a collaborative learning process to help their organizations meet the challenges of a complex and chaotic work environment. Unlike traditional mentors, new managerial mentors serve as both teachers and learners in a relationship based on shared purpose, co-inquiry, respect, and trust.

Chapter One links the need for organizational transformation to the concept of the learning organization. It provides an overview of the characteristics of the typical learning organization and an assessment tool for determining the extent to which an organization possesses those characteristics.

Chapter Two details the new mentoring relationship and why it fits the needs of today's turbulent organizations better than the currently popular concept of the free agent. It describes how managerial mentors as learning leaders can

3

navigate a difficult course between leading and learning in such a way that leading facilitates learning and learning fosters leading.

Chapter Three provides an introduction to the diverse competencies of the learning leader. It outlines four managerial roles—Collaborator, Innovator, Producer, and Integrator—and shows how the competencies associated with each of those roles are essential to learning leadership. A Learning Leader Role Preference Inventory provides insight into an individual's current managerial role preferences and serves as an introduction to the full role descriptions in Part Two.

CHAPTER ONE

# From Managing to Mentoring

IF YOU SENSE THAT PROFOUND CHANGES are taking place in your organization, you're right! Large and small organizations in every corner of the world are struggling to survive in what management writer Peter Vaill (1989) calls a "permanent white water" environment. Traditionally conservative banks and insurance companies in the United States are trying to keep up with changing government regulations and move aggressively into new markets. Manufacturers are trying to cope with the threat of increasingly stiff global competition. The health care industry is mired in a transition to managed care that is creating an angry backlash from health care professionals and the general public.

While most everyone is feeling the impact of chaotic organizational change, few people feel prepared to cope with change, let alone make it work for them. Over thirty years ago, organizational theorists Bennis, Benne, and Chin (1961) published one of the first major books on organizational change, *The Planning of Change*. Written for less-turbulent times, the visions and strategies they presented were widely adopted. Now, in what management author Charles Handy (1994) has characterized as the Age of Paradox, the notion of planned change seems almost archaic. Organizational leaders are realizing that the old change strategies are inadequate for survival in "permanent white water" and that the times call for a radical transformation in the ways that people think and work together.

## The Learning Connection

In a *Harvard Business Review* article, Chris Argyris (1991) warns that while success in the marketplace calls for continual learning, most people don't know how to learn and those who are often thought to be the best learners are, in fact, poor at it.

Traditionally, organizations placed more emphasis on training than on learning. Learning was viewed as something that happened at school, not at work. The learning that did take place usually had more to do with the past than the future. All that has changed in the last few years, however, since the "learning organization" has become the latest management fad. Unlike some management fads, the learning organization is not a product but a complex set of processes that make it difficult to define. Pedler, Burgoyne, and Boydell (1991) describe a learning organization as one that continuously transforms itself by facilitating the learning of all its members. The implication is that individuals in learning organizations engage in continual learning in order to generate new ideas that enable organizations to sustain a competitive edge in an uncertain marketplace.

In spite of the current enthusiasm for the concept of the learning organization, there is concern that it will suffer the

fate of other potentially transformative management initiatives. Like quality, the learning organization can be integral to
organizational survival over the long term. But, as has happened with many quality initiatives, organizations that take a
superficial view of what is involved in the way of new work
designs and different managerial practices will not become
learning organizations. A learning organization cannot be
imposed on traditional hierarchies.

In one sense, every organization that adapts to a changing
environment is learning, but adaptation does not make it a
learning organization. What distinguishes the learning organization is that at both the individual and organizational level
it actively engages in the search for new knowledge that is
continually shared and used to create more learning. Learning, in other words, becomes what Peter Vaill (1996) calls "a
way of being."

Assessment 1 on pages 8—9 will allow you to take a
quick overview of the extent to which your organization possesses some of the characteristics of a learning organization.
It is not a comprehensive or necessarily valid instrument. It
is instead intended to give you a rough idea of some of the
systems and processes that characterize a typical learning
organization.

If your organization scores 70 or higher on the assessment
rating scale, you are working in an environment that possesses many of the characteristics of a learning organization. If the
score is 30 or lower, look at your individual item scores to try
to identify some actions that you might take to create more of
a learning focus in your organization. Keep in mind that
while all of the assessment items have been associated with
typical learning organizations, a particular action may or may
not be a good fit for your organization at this time. The

## ASSESSMENT 1: **LEARNING ORGANIZATION ASSESSMENT**

*Directions:* Decide what organizational unit you want to assess. It can be your entire organization, a division, a department, or a work unit as long as the unit has an identifiable leader or leaders. Rate each of the statements below based on how true that statement is of your organization. After you have rated all twenty statements, add the column subtotals and total them. Mark the grand total score on the scale at the end of the assessment.

|  | Not true | | | | Very true |
|---|---|---|---|---|---|
| 1. Leaders communicate a clear vision of the organization's future. | 1 | 2 | 3 | 4 | 5 |
| 2. Work processes are updated to meet changing marketplace needs. | 1 | 2 | 3 | 4 | 5 |
| 3. People share best practices with others in the organization. | 1 | 2 | 3 | 4 | 5 |
| 4. Win/lose competition among teams is discouraged. | 1 | 2 | 3 | 4 | 5 |
| 5. Long-term people are valued for their knowledge of the organization. | 1 | 2 | 3 | 4 | 5 |
| 6. Leaders promote workforce diversity as a competitive advantage. | 1 | 2 | 3 | 4 | 5 |
| 7. Work flow analyses are done to improve intergroup coordination. | 1 | 2 | 3 | 4 | 5 |
| 8. People build relationships through networking. | 1 | 2 | 3 | 4 | 5 |
| 9. Teams are self-managed. | 1 | 2 | 3 | 4 | 5 |
| 10. People set their own learning goals. | 1 | 2 | 3 | 4 | 5 |

|  | Not true | | | | Very true |
|---|---|---|---|---|---|
| 11. Leaders promote innovation and risk taking. | 1 | 2 | 3 | 4 | 5 |
| 12. New information technology is used to improve work systems. | 1 | 2 | 3 | 4 | 5 |
| 13. Periodic feedback is solicited from key stakeholders. | 1 | 2 | 3 | 4 | 5 |
| 14. Teams practice creative problem solving. | 1 | 2 | 3 | 4 | 5 |
| 15. Managers coach and mentor people. | 1 | 2 | 3 | 4 | 5 |
| 16. Leaders personally model espoused organizational values. | 1 | 2 | 3 | 4 | 5 |
| 17. Job designs allow for personal initiative and judgment. | 1 | 2 | 3 | 4 | 5 |
| 18. People are encouraged to raise controversial issues for discussion. | 1 | 2 | 3 | 4 | 5 |
| 19. Cross-functional teams are created for special projects. | 1 | 2 | 3 | 4 | 5 |
| 20. Interpersonal skills are as highly valued as technical skills. | 1 | 2 | 3 | 4 | 5 |

**Column totals** _ _ _ _ _

**Grand total** _____

**Rating scale:**

0     20     40     60     80     100

purpose of the assessment tool is to get you thinking about what is involved in building a learning organization and what kinds of things you might do to begin or enhance the process in your organization.

Experienced managers in today's organizations find themselves in the paradoxical position of having acquired much technical know-how over the years but knowing less than many younger people in the organization. Given that reality, managerial mentors need to broaden their skill base, particularly in the area of learning leadership.

In a learning organization, individuals take personal responsibility for their own learning. For managers, facilitating learning replaces control as the core management task. Individual and organizational learning is critical to survival in a permanent white-water situation. Learning, in this sense, means expanding both individual and organizational capacity to do new things. Learning and doing are no longer viewed as separate activities but are integrated as people interact and reflect together on what works, what needs to be changed, and why. Interaction with others is vital because only through the process of nonjudgmental dialogue does it become possible for people to bring to the surface the different assumptions that lead to misunderstanding, conflict, and resistance to change.

In *Real Change Leaders,* Katzenbach and the RCL Team (1995) suggest that while becoming a change leader requires hard work and the acquisition of new skills, the managers who succeed at it say they do it for the satisfaction of helping others grow. Such change leaders are also very performance focused and results driven. Their value to the organization lies in their ability to integrate tough performance standards with an in-depth understanding of their marketplace and the organization's growth plans. Managers who possess the skills to motivate, mentor, and engage in collaborative learning can serve as exemplary leaders of change.

## The New Managerial Mentor

Managers are coming to the painful realization that there are no one-minute solutions to today's complex problems. As a result, experienced managers are frantically casting about for ways to cope with unbridled change and a fractious work-force. In the words of one frustrated senior manager in a recently merged large bank in the Southwest:

> This place really used to care about people. . . . We were like a family, and top management supported us in giving back to the community and going the extra mile for our customers. . . . Since the merger it's been dog-eat-dog. . . . They brought in a whole bunch of executives who don't know anything about the business and couldn't care less about the customers. . . . We spend all of our time in computer classes learning about systems that fail to work. . . . My people are constantly in my face to do something, and I can't tell them that it won't make any difference because corporate says they're probably going to get rid of all the branches soon anyway. (Client communication)

This bank manager's discouragement is certainly not unique to the financial services industry. Regardless of industry, size, or sector, managers as a whole are running scared. As managers find themselves caught in the crosshairs of the shift from hierarchical to horizontal organizational structures, they hear management gurus predict the end of management as we have known it for the last century. In the midst of all this uncertainty, managers find themselves forced to take on more work under stressful conditions for fewer rewards. It is no wonder that large numbers of people are disenchanted.

Instead of heightening managerial anxiety by predicting the impending disappearance of middle management through reengineering and de-layering, more emphasis should be placed on helping managers understand what Harvard Business School professor Rosabeth Moss Kanter (1983) calls the "new managerial work." She points out the need for managers to shift from acting as watchdogs and interventionists to serving as integrators and facilitators. While Kanter and others stop short of specifically trying to describe the managerial job of the future, it is clear that the new managers will be doing fundamentally different things and will therefore need to redefine their jobs and develop new competencies. Successful managerial mentors will break through traditional job boundaries and find new ways to add value to their organizations. That will require a new managerial mind-set.

The new managerial mentor will need to learn how to think outside of the "job box." William Bridges (1994), the author of JobShift, describes jobs as "boxes of activity" bounded by job descriptions. He stresses that workers will need to prepare for what he calls a "dejobbed" world in the twenty-first century. He predicts that jobs as we now know them will be a thing of the past and that the way to get out of the job box is to start looking at everything as a market: "In a market . . . people don't have bosses or supervisors . . . one has customers. . . . According to the market paradigm, one's boss is really a major customer rather than an authority in the old sense" (p. 64).

In dejobbed organizations, managers no longer direct the work of people in "jobs." As managerial mentors, they facilitate new learning. They are responsible for helping people develop a full understanding of the organization's strategy, goals, and values so that each individual will have a clear picture of how his or her work adds value to the organization.

Managerial mentors must first learn how to break out of their own job boxes in order to become learning leaders. They must replace their traditional control-based practices with new working collaborations designed to meet customer needs in a changing marketplace. Their focus is on helping individuals and teams engage in continual learning to identify what they can do, what they want to do, and what they must do to make the optimum contribution to their organizations.

An excellent way for you to start getting out of your job box is to take a fresh look at how you approach your work. British management consultant and writer Rosemary Stewart (1982) has developed a useful framework for analyzing managerial work. Based on extensive research, Stewart found that all managerial positions offer choice in *what* can be done as well as *how* it can be done. In her view, much attention has been paid to the latter, but little to the former. Stewart's framework has three parts: *demands*—what an individual must do; *constraints*—factors that limit what an individual can do; and *choices*—activities that an individual can do but does not have to do. Demands, constraints, and choices are dynamic in that they change over time.

Chances are that you approach your work in your own way, both in terms of what you focus on and how you do it. Stewart's framework is particularly helpful because it shows how to step outside of the job box and take an objective view of your work focus. According to Stewart, most people tend to emphasize some parts of their work more than others—one manager may focus more on the technical aspects, another on administration. In *Choices for the Manager,* Stewart (1982) argues that managers who work in what she calls "flexible domains" need to take a more strategic view of what they *can* do. Stewart's work seems prophetic now, more than fifteen years later, as virtually all managers struggle to work effectively in "flexible domains."

While the ensuing chapters will provide you with the comprehensive tools you will need to develop a managerial mentoring strategy, the questions in Exercise 1 will help you look at whether you may be stuck in a job box. After you have answered all nine items on the checklist, go back and make some notes to yourself about actions you might take to address specific items.

The checklist will help you think more strategically about your work. Like most busy managers, you probably get so involved in doing your work that you don't step out of it long enough to take an objective look at the value you are adding to the business. Stewart's research showed that people tend to approach their work in ways that come naturally to them and that, as a result, they miss some of the potential for choice. By taking a strategic perspective, you will be able to make more informed choices and increase your effectiveness to the organization.

## The New Managerial Mentor as Learning Leader

Every organization has people who possess special knowledge or expertise that is invaluable to the organization. These individuals might be research scientists, technical experts, or customer service representatives. Some of them work independently, others consult to the rest of the organization. Still

## EXERCISE 1: **WORK STRATEGY CHECKLIST**

|  | Yes | No |
|---|---|---|
| 1. Do you align your work strategy with changing organizational needs? | _____ | _____ |
| 2. Do you regularly review the effectiveness of your work outcomes? | _____ | _____ |
| 3. Do you push the boundaries of your job description? | _____ | _____ |
| 4. Do important tasks take precedence over urgent tasks? | _____ | _____ |
| 5. Do you feel energized by your work? | _____ | _____ |
| 6. Do you have a support network at work? | _____ | _____ |
| 7. Do you look for new ways to do things? | _____ | _____ |
| 8. Do you maintain useful external contacts? | _____ | _____ |
| 9. Do you build relationships up, down, and across the organization? | _____ | _____ |

others manage business units or use their special know-how to solve customer problems. One thing many of them have in common is their desire to share their learning and facilitate the learning of others.

Many of these experienced managers and professionals want to mentor others. They differ from traditional mentors in that they do not want to teach, instruct, or train; they want to collaborate with others in the learning process. Their goal is to bring thinking and doing together and through their joint efforts expand individual and team capacity in ways that add value to the organization.

These potential managerial mentors usually share another invaluable quality: institutional memory. Having been a part of their organizations for some time, they have seen a lot of change and know what has been tried, what has worked, and what has failed. In *The Future of Leadership*, White, Hodgson, and Crainer (1996) describe the need for a new kind of learning leader: "White-water leaders will identify productive areas of uncertainty and confusion and lead the organization into those areas in order to gain competitive or other kinds of advantage. They will do so with role models that always contain some radical elements which emphasize the importance of utilizing and leveraging learning, personally and organizationally" (p. 88).

White and his coauthors liken learning leaders to experienced travelers. Like knowledgeable managers and professionals, experienced travelers know that there are different ways to reach their destination, and they use their experience and the experience of others to learn and adapt to unforeseen circumstances and take advantage of new opportunities. The new managerial mentor is that kind of learning leader.

To become a learning leader, you will need to leverage your personal learning through the acquisition of new competencies. Your role will be to bridge the gap between individual and organizational learning. By supporting and stretching the learning abilities of those around you, you can use your institutional wisdom to help create the kind of learning environment that will move your organization into the next century. M.I.T.'s Peter Senge (1990b) describes the new roles of learning leaders as designers, teachers, and stewards. He stresses that these roles will require managers to develop new skills in visioning, in challenging existing mental models, and in fostering systemic thinking.

Becoming a learning leader is not an easy task. It will require you to take a hard look at your current skills, the needs of the organization, and the learning that you will need to do to bridge the gap. It will require you to take some risks—a tough thing to do in an uncertain organizational environment where many people are threatened by change.

Efforts at organizational change are more likely to succeed if organizations actively develop managerial change leaders. Therein lies a golden opportunity for you as a manager or professional: By becoming a new managerial mentor, you can serve as a critical linchpin for learning in your organization.

CHAPTER TWO

# The New Mentoring Relationship

DOUGLAS HALL AND ASSOCIATES (1994), a widely respected group of career theorists and practitioners, titled their most recent book *The Career Is Dead—Long Live the Career*. Their message is that the career as we have known it—"a series of upward moves with steadily increasing income, power, status, and security (p. 1)"—is a thing of the past. The old view of career development based on individual mastery has been replaced by what Hall calls the relational approach to careers. Hall and his colleagues propose that the primary resources for career development in today's turbulent work settings are job challenges and relationships with others. Given the multitude of challenges facing today's managers, the key to career survival lies in identifying new ways to engage in collaborative learning.

In the current environment, career development is a mutual process in which the traditional mentor-protégé relationship is replaced by what Hall calls "co-learning." In today's workplace, where junior managers often have more expertise in certain areas, such as new technologies, than their seniors, co-learning becomes essential. In Hall's relational model, interdependence replaces independence as the object of growth. The model also includes the concept of reciprocity, the expectation that "both parties to a developmental relationship will possess the skills to function as interdependent co-learners and that they will be motivated to use these skills" (p. 3). Unlike the traditional mentor-protégé relationship, either party can be the teacher or the learner, and the focus is on co-inquiry.

Many management writers have chronicled the changing psychological contract between workers and their organizations. Some CEOs, including Jack Welch of General Electric, say that the old psychological contract, based on continued employment in exchange for loyalty and hard work, has been replaced by a one-day contract based on the current value that each party brings to the relationship. While some organizations support that view, other leading-edge companies define the new contract in terms of how well an individual meets customer needs, engages in continual learning, and adapts to change. In exchange, the organization offers developmental learning opportunities and performance-based rewards.

Much has been written in the past few years about the concept of "free agency." Tom Peters (1997) promotes something similar called "Me Inc": "Forget your job title. Ask yourself: What do I do that adds remarkable, measurable, distinguished, distinctive value? Forget your job description. Ask yourself: What do I do that I am most proud of? Most of all, forget about the standard rungs of progression you've climbed in your career up to now" (p. 86).

Many current career success books and manuals echo Peters's message. Given the anger, fear, and disillusionment caused by massive corporate downsizing and the violation of the traditional psychological contract, the popularity of the me-first view is understandable. Taken to the extreme, however, excessive self-promotion can undermine the critical need for collaboration and co-learning. While Peters is really addressing the need for people to learn how to market themselves, the risk is that disaffected managers will hear it as a rationale for devoting all of one's energies to promoting oneself. This is unfortunate because in a rapidly changing work environment, no one individual can possibly have all the answers. Connecting and collaborating with others to keep abreast of change and make midcourse corrections is needed to achieve success in turbulent times.

Hall and Associates (1994) say that what is needed is a relational contract based on business success, clarity of purpose, mutual connection, respect, and trust. While "pack your own parachute" remains a popular theme among managers, one also hears a concurrent call for meaningful work in ethical organizations that will treat people fairly in exchange for the chance to learn and grow with the business. Over the long haul, pure free agency will not work because there will be too little commitment to shared organizational goals. One can already see the negative effects of unbridled free agency in the sports industry in the grandstanding of pampered athletes and the horse trading of team owners. As a work ethic, free agency leaves much to be desired. As long as employees are eager to jump ship for a few dollars and organizations have no second thoughts about letting people go after years of committed service, there can be no foundation for mutual trust and collaboration.

The positive side of free agency lies in its emphasis on personal responsibility. In the current work environment, job survival is contingent on knowing one's talents and using them to work both independently and interdependently. A major problem, however, is that it is not particularly easy for managers to become flexible, self-directed free agents. Traditional managers find it hard to let go of the old psychological contract and continue to look to top management to tell them what to do. In order for the co-learning relationship to work for them, organizations will need to provide learning opportunities to help traditional managers develop a new mind-set about the value of collaborative learning.

New managerial mentors who view the co-learning relationship as a challenge rather than a threat will help themselves and their organizations move successfully into the next century. By focusing on emerging business needs and learning how to take the initiative, they can create new roles for themselves as active leaders of change. As learning leaders, these managerial mentors are well-positioned to promote and model the behaviors needed to refocus people's energies and build the collaborative relationships needed for future organizational excellence.

## Rethinking Change

Effective leaders of change are both results driven and committed to helping people achieve and grow on the job. They understand the organization's mission and vision and are constantly on the lookout for new ways to improve performance. Research by Katzenbach and the RCL Team (1995) demonstrated that, contrary to conventional wisdom, the make-or-break factor in successful organizational change is not top management but middle managers. These researchers showed how middle managers create positive change by acting as linchpins between customers, employees, and top management.

Learning leaders view change as an ongoing reality. Instead of trying to "make" change happen, managerial mentors facilitate the process by helping people reach their full potential. They assess current reality and seek ways to release the natural energies of people. By engaging in dialogue and reflection, they help people learn how to work together in ways that enable change to occur naturally. This approach is based on the assumption that change cannot be "managed" in a controlled way when there are many unpredictable elements in the system.

Some change agents have acted on the assumption that in chaotic times, a "bottom-up" approach to change makes more sense than a "top-down" approach. Unfortunately, both types of change efforts have often proved disappointing. One difficulty with "bottom-up" programs is that they frequently lack focus and are not adequately targeted at critical business priorities. Another problem, cited earlier, is that traditionalist managers, with their penchant for stability and role clarity, find it difficult to work in the absence of clear marching orders from the top. As Heckscher (1995) points out in *White Collar Blues*, for the last fifty years the traditional employment relationship has called for near total lifetime security in exchange for near total subordination to the corporate will. The old paternalism, which gave comfort and stability to traditionalist managers for many years, does not die easily.

If neither top-down nor bottom-up approaches work, what is a viable model for organizational change? In the more than one hundred international organizations researched by

Binney and Williams (1995), successful leaders of change were those who went beyond either alternative and practiced both strong, directive leadership and a commitment to learning. On the one hand, they did not assume that change would happen naturally; they directed people's energies to key business issues and priorities. On the other hand, they did not force change down people's throats; they encouraged people to take the initiative, exercise autonomy, and learn by doing. In the words of Binney and Williams: "These leaders combine clear direction with creating space for others to take initiative; they are straight talking, forthright and yet highly effective listeners. In their hands providing direction and allowing autonomy, being forthright and listening are not contradictory; they are complementary" (p. 7).

Assertive leadership and responsiveness to the needs and interests of others reinforce one another. It is *because* effective learning leaders have a strong belief in what they are doing that they are able to relate to others and provide the boundaries within which people can act independently. Effective learning leaders view directive leadership and responsiveness to others as two sides of the same coin. They navigate a difficult course between leading and learning in such a way that leading facilitates learning and learning fosters leading.

Learning leadership can be practiced by managerial mentors to set high performance goals and build good relationships. Because they are on the front lines and are accountable for producing results, the new managerial mentors can promote change, encourage people to take charge of their careers, and find meaning in their work. Navigating the course between leading and learning is the key challenge for the new managerial mentor. It calls for acquiring and practicing diverse managerial roles and competencies that go well beyond what is typically taught in management development class-rooms.

## The Changing Managerial Paradigm

In a classic *Harvard Business Review* article, Abraham Zaleznik (1977) contrasted leaders and managers. He depicted managers as impersonal, operationally focused problem solvers and leaders as intuitive, people-oriented risk takers. Since that time, many well-known management writers— among them Kanter (1983), Tichy (1997), Maccoby (1988), and Bennis (1997)—have written extensively on leadership. A common theme today is that managerial leadership is needed at *all* levels if organizations are going to be successful in transitional times.

Robert Quinn (1986), the author of *Deep Change,* describes the traditional paradigm of what he calls "political transaction." The underlying premise of this paradigm is per-sonal survival, and managers exchange resources through negotiation and compromise. They use rational persuasion to get what they want and when that fails, they employ political tactics. They tend to avoid risk taking and try to avoid con-frontation with authority figures. Feeling intense pressure to conform, transactional managers will not do anything to rock the boat even when they become aware of the need for change. As organizational loyalists, they expect the people at the top to know what needs to be done.

Quinn offers an alternative organizational paradigm that he calls the "transformational paradigm." Rather than person-al survival, the underlying premise here is the realization of a personal vision grounded in moral rather than political values. In the transformational paradigm, the organization is viewed not as a technical or political system but as a system in which certain values and principles are more powerful than the political interests of any particular coalition. In order to internalize the transformational paradigm, managers must first undergo deep personal change. They must become internally driven leaders who see beyond technical competence and political exchange. They must be driven by learning and the desire to realize a personal vision. CEOs are not the only possible transformational leaders; transformational leaders can be developed at all levels of an organization. Our new managerial mentor, who models the change process for others, closely resembles Quinn's transformational leader.

Because organizational change stirs up intense emotion, people need help in coping with threat and maintaining their self-esteem under difficult conditions. Until managers see the value to themselves and their organizations of becoming learning leaders and helping people understand the "whys" of change, the victim mentality will prevail and productivity will suffer. Organizations have implemented a variety of programs to help managers become active facilitators of change, but many of these programs are either overly conceptual or place too much emphasis on manager-as-counselor.

Transaction-oriented managers are ill-equipped to deal with the emotional fallout of traumatic organizational change. For them, emotions have no part in informed management decision making. Managerial mentors should not be expected to play a semitherapeutic role. The support they provide should be work focused and designed to help people stop seeing themselves as victims and instead become self-directed learners engaged in meaningful work. These new managerial mentors have a critical role to play in helping their organizations translate strategy into action. As twenty-first-century organizations become flatter, managerial mentors will be the learning leaders who operate where the hierarchical and the horizontal meet.

In *The Drama of Leadership*, Patricia Pitcher (1997) writes about the destructive influence of the technocratic mentality. Pitcher has extensive hands-on management experience and has been a member of the board of directors of several major corporations. Her book, based on an eight-year study of organizational leaders, explodes many management myths about what represents good leadership. She refutes the notion that leaders are in short supply and shows that many potential leaders go unrecognized or unappreciated.

Pitcher provides numerous examples of the destructive impact of technocratic managers who lack the vision and humanity needed in today's organizations. She identifies three types of leaders: artists, who are visionary, intuitive, and people oriented; craftsmen, who are humane, dedicated, and wise; and technocrats, who are brilliant, well-schooled in the latest theory, detail oriented, rigid, methodical, and self-centered. In her view, technocrats are typically seen as the people with leadership talent, yet her research demonstrates that their failure to understand the human side of the equation usually has a devastating effect on organizational effectiveness. Pitcher recommends that organizations cultivate the leadership talents of underutilized artists and craftsmen. If we want to create true learning organizations, she says, we must go beyond the technocratic mentality that permeates organization life.

In contrast to the above description of the narrow-minded technocrat, Pitcher describes the managerial mind-set of the craftsman: "Managing organizations and managing people is a Craft. Not an Art and most certainly not a Science.

**27**

Rejuvenating organizations may be an Art. Managing things, or thing-like aspects of organizations, may be a Science. But the Craft of managing people takes wisdom, patience, experience, authority, conviction, realism" (p. 200).

In less-chaotic times, the technocratic approach worked well and managers were rewarded more for their brain power than for their human skills. In fact, that is still the case in some high-tech settings. But in organizations where teamwork and creativity are required, a new breed is emerging. These are the[learning leaders who are breaking new ground by combining a strong performance orientation with a talent for motivating and challenging people to get in tune with the changing marketplace.] The strength of these new managerial mentors lies in their ability to achieve high performance by getting people to change their behaviors to better satisfy customer needs.

Learning leaders think and act differently than traditional managers. They are not afraid to get involved in the real work of their units and do not bury themselves in endless analyses. They are willing to take risks. They welcome change and the opportunity to take on new challenges. Because they are often mavericks by nature, they tend to be unappreciated by their more traditional associates. As a result, many of these innovative producers either quit in frustration or are forced out of their organizations. This is unfortunate because they are the very individuals who possess many of the learning leader qualities needed to help their organizations move successfully into the next century. In the next chapter, you will be introduced to those learning leader qualities.

CHAPTER THREE

# The Diverse Competencies
# of the Learning Leader

A COMPETENCY IS THE KNOWLEDGE, ability, or skill required to perform a given task or role. A role is not the same thing as a job description. A job description is essentially a static collection of job tasks; a role is dynamic and has to do with the personal meaning people put on their work and the choices they make about their contribution and their relationships with others. This does not mean that roles have no specific task requirements; managers are traditionally involved in the transactional tasks of planning, organizing, and directing. The distinction has more to do with how managers see themselves and how they are seen by others in the organization. As demonstrated by Stewart's (1982) research described in Chapter One, managers can make choices about whether they want to view the job narrowly or exploit the opportunities inherent in the managerial role to make a more meaningful contribution to the organization and their own learning.

This definition of a competency implies that knowledge alone is insufficient for high-quality managerial performance. In times of turbulent change, performance excellence calls for a wide-ranging repertoire of well-honed managerial skills. Managerial mentors, with their combination of knowledge and specific expertise, are well-positioned to become leaders of change if they are able to redefine and broaden their perception of their managerial roles.

Our competency model for the new managerial mentor draws directly on Quinn's (1996) research on CEOs described in *Deep Change*. He describes four managerial roles—Vision Setter, Motivator, Analyzer, and Taskmaster—with the first two roles labeled as *transformational* and the last two as *transactional* in nature. Quinn contends that all four managerial roles are critical to effective managerial performance, and that in times of change, the transformational roles are especially important. He thinks that managers need to broaden their perception of their roles and take a wider view of their jobs.

In *Deep Change*, Quinn displays the four CEO roles in the form of a matrix. The graphic in Figure 1 depicting the roles and competencies of the new managerial mentor is an adaptation of Quinn's CEO matrix. His concept of competing transactional and transformational leadership roles zeroes in on the roles and competencies of the managerial mentor as learning leader. Like Quinn's, our graphic of the managerial mentor comprises four roles—Collaborator, Innovator, Producer, and Integrator—with three learning leader competencies associated with each role. With learning leadership at the center, the endpoints of the vertical and horizontal axes, respectively, depict roles that are transformational or transactional in nature, or infrastructure or marketplace focused. All

Figure 1. **Role Competencies of the New Managerial Mentor**

**TRANSFORMATIONAL**

| **ROLE:** Collaborator | **ROLE:** Innovator |
| **FOCUS:** Relationships | **FOCUS:** Change |
| **COMPETENCIES:** Facilitating Coaching Dialoguing | **COMPETENCIES:** Visioning Championing Diffusing |

**INFRASTRUCTURE** ◄ **Learning Leadership** ► **MARKETPLACE**

| **ROLE:** Integrator | **ROLE:** Producer |
| **FOCUS:** Alignment | **FOCUS:** Results |
| **COMPETENCIES:** Organizing Improving Bridging | **COMPETENCIES:** Targeting Improvising Measuring |

**TRANSACTIONAL**

four roles are integral to successful managerial mentoring, based on our belief that both technical and interpersonal excellence are essential in today's complex organizational settings. Some situations may call for structure, others for flexibility, and still others for both, such as organizations that are expanding and downsizing at the same time. Managers must become proficient in all the competencies needed to meet the demands of a rapidly changing marketplace.

Organizations of all kinds are realizing that in today's complex world, collaboration is the most productive way to think and work together. The shift from "I" to "we" thinking is happening at all organizational levels, from internal project teams to collaborative ventures between large organizations such as Microsoft and Intel. Collaboration represents a major cultural transformation from isolation and individualism to interaction and cooperation among people in every area of human endeavor. Since the evidence shows that old hierarchies and boundaries do not dissolve easily, however, the managerial mentoring role of Collaborator is essential to helping people find new and better ways to relate to each other and to key stakeholders.

The three Collaborator competencies of Facilitating, Coaching, and Dialoguing provide learning leaders with a relational model for engaging the creative talents of everyone around a shared purpose. Organizations have espoused the value of teamwork for years, but too often the primary focus is on interpersonal skill building rather than knowledge sharing and collaborative problem solving. As a result, the critical connection between work team effectiveness and organizational results is not made. While the role of Collaborator is essential to learning leadership, it is only one of two transformational mentoring roles.

The second role, Innovator, goes hand in hand with that of Collaborator in its focus on organizational transformation. The managerial mentor who practices the Innovator competencies of Visioning, Championing, and Diffusing is very different from the stereotype of isolated ivory-tower thinker or flamboyant entrepreneur. As learning leaders, Innovators collaborate with others in the organization to find creative solutions that promote change.

Innovators are primarily focused on the marketplace and how to develop breakthrough products and services to gain the competitive edge. They are real-world visionaries who actively network to get their ideas heard and accepted. They are energized by collaborative thinking and, as politically astute learning leaders, they know that an innovation is only an idea until it is implemented. With their focus on the external marketplace, Innovators are less concerned with organizational infrastructures but, unlike ivory-tower types, know that they must concern themselves with the alignment of internal systems and structures if they want their innovations to work. Therefore, they will do what is required to support the integration process.

Unlike the Collaborator and Innovator roles, the third managerial mentoring role of Producer is transactional. It comprises the competencies needed to get results—Targeting, Improvising, and Measuring—which resemble traditional managerial goal-setting and monitoring tasks. As learning leaders, however, Producers are not obsessed solely with the numbers. They are constantly on the alert for new targets to meet emerging marketplace needs and regularly provide progress data to help people see the results of their efforts.

Producers use every opportunity to motivate others and are quick to recognize and reward outstanding performance.

Unlike the stereotype of the autocratic whip-cracking manager, Producers balance a strong results orientation with an emphasis on collaboration and team spirit. They capitalize on the fun of working and learning together. Because they are extremely task driven, they sometimes get frustrated about the time required to process and negotiate relationships, but as competent learning leaders, they know that they must spend the time up front to get the results they want.

Integrator, the fourth managerial mentoring role, focuses on the alignment of organizational systems and structures. Also a transactional role, it relates to the traditional management competencies of Organizing, Improving, and Bridging, but with a difference. As learning leaders, Integrators do not rely on reorganization as the primary change strategy. They are less concerned with spans of control and organization charts than with how to build organizational designs that encourage people to network across organizational lines and engage in creative collaboration. Integrators work with people to design motivating, customer-focused jobs that foster continual learning on the job.

Integrators initiate process improvement programs not because they are the latest management fad but because they provide a way to add value for the customer. They serve as bridges who link broad-based organizational strategy with internal support systems. In times of change, they help bring the best of the past into the future. As learning leaders, they make appropriate use of new technologies to enhance coordination and cooperation across organizational boundaries. They act as stabilizers to ensure that the appropriate organizational designs are in place to support continual learning and transformational change.

## The Learning Leader Role
## Preference Inventory

By way of introduction, complete the inventory (pages 36 — 39) presented in Assessment 2 to informally assess yourself in the four managerial role competency areas. The inventory addresses your expressed preferences in each role competency area. It has nothing to do with your current or potential skill level in any of them. After you have completed the inventory, total your scores on the scoring sheet (on page 40) and make a mental note of your relative highs and lows in each of the four role competency areas. Remember, the inventory is an informal assessment and is intended only to provide you with a rough idea of your baseline preferences and to serve as an introduction to the full role competency descriptions in later chapters.

Before you move on to the descriptions of the four competing roles of the managerial mentor, think about your own significant learning experiences. Were they in training programs or on the job? Were they experiences that capitalized on your strong skills or did they require you to learn new things? Did you choose those experiences or were they assigned to you by others? Chances are they were experiences that presented you with a difficult challenge and required you to perform in areas where you had to learn by doing, possibly under adverse conditions. If you were able to successfully master those situations, you probably look back on them now as invaluable learning experiences because they forced you to move out of your comfort zone and take a new look at yourself.

In order to become a learning leader, you first have to become a learner yourself and develop the competencies to become a managerial mentor. Once you have created your

ASSESSMENT 2: **LEARNING LEADER ROLE PREFERENCE INVENTORY**

*Directions:* For each of the following items, assign four (4) points to your top choice, three (3) points to your second choice, two (2) points to your third choice, and one (1) point to your least-preferred choice,

|  | **Points** |
|---|---|
| 1. The most important factor in the success of a business is | |
|     a. efficient operations | _____ |
|     b. committed people | _____ |
|     c. a clear vision of the future | _____ |
|     d. challenging goals | _____ |
| 2. When things get chaotic in my unit, I | |
|     a. look for creative solutions | _____ |
|     b. provide encouragement and support | _____ |
|     c. take prompt and decisive action | _____ |
|     d. analyze the causes of the problem | _____ |
| 3. I prefer organizational change that is | |
|     a. planned and incremental | _____ |
|     b. innovative and wide ranging | _____ |
|     c. targeted and results oriented | _____ |
|     d. focused on learning and personal growth | _____ |
| 4. I particularly enjoy | |
|     a. building collaborative teams | _____ |
|     b. promoting new ideas to higher-ups | _____ |
|     c. achieving impressive results | _____ |
|     d. developing improved systems | _____ |
| 5. My typical approach to decision making is to | |
|     a. explore innovative solutions | _____ |
|     b. take the most practical course of action | _____ |
|     c. collaborate with team members | _____ |
|     d. systematically evaluate alternatives | _____ |

6. The best way to prepare for an unpredictable future is to
   a. reengineer        _____
   b. help people learn how to cope with change        _____
   c. create a tangible vision        _____
   d. achieve current objectives        _____

7. My most important job should be to
   a. improve operating efficiency        _____
   b. meet performance goals        _____
   c. build effective teams        _____
   d. find new ways to satisfy customers        _____

8. I try to optimize individual performance by
   a. coaching and developing people        _____
   b. using personal motivation techniques        _____
   c. creating more interesting job designs        _____
   d. championing change as a career opportunity        _____

9. It is most important for people to have
   a. the tools to get the job done        _____
   b. high motivation to achieve        _____
   c. cooperative and friendly co-workers        _____
   d. the ability to cope with change        _____

10. My preferred stage in project work is
    a. generating new ideas        _____
    b. designing work flow        _____
    c. team building        _____
    d. goal setting        _____

11. The main purpose of networking is to
    a. build new relationships        _____
    b. use influence to get results        _____
    c. solve coordination problems between units        _____
    d. broker support for new initiatives        _____

12. In problem-solving sessions, I like to
    a. brainstorm new ideas _____
    b. encourage group dialogue _____
    c. promote expedient solutions _____
    d. map out the problem _____

13. The most critical element in team development is
    a. conflict management _____
    b. defined roles and responsibilities _____
    c. breakthrough thinking _____
    d. performance focus _____

14. I tend to think of myself as a
    a. conceptualizer _____
    b. relater _____
    c. analyzer _____
    d. doer _____

15. I prefer to motivate people with
    a. an exciting vision of the future _____
    b. opportunities for personal development _____
    c. special rewards and recognition _____
    d. stretch goals _____

16. I get great satisfaction from
    a. helping people learn _____
    b. exploring new marketplace needs _____
    c. implementing quality initiatives _____
    d. achieving performance expectations _____

17. People tend to see me as
    a. driven _____
    b. efficient _____
    c. creative _____
    d. supportive _____

18. My typical interpersonal style is
    a. analytic           _____
    b. direct             _____
    c. empathic           _____
    d. charismatic        _____

19. Businesses should place the greatest importance on
    a. human learning potential    _____
    b. breakthrough technology     _____
    c. strong leadership           _____
    d. quality systems             _____

20. The people I work best with are
    a. technically oriented    _____
    b. innovative              _____
    c. action driven           _____
    d. collaborative           _____

## Learning Leader Role Preference Scoring Sheet

*Record your point assignments for each item and add up your totals for each of the four columns. Your highest column total indicates your most preferred role. Look at your lowest score. That may be the role on which you most need to focus your development efforts.*

| Item | Collaborator | Innovator | Producer | Integrator |
|---|---|---|---|---|
| 1. | b ____ | c ____ | d ____ | a ____ |
| 2. | b ____ | a ____ | c ____ | d ____ |
| 3. | d ____ | b ____ | c ____ | a ____ |
| 4. | a ____ | b ____ | c ____ | d ____ |
| 5. | c ____ | a ____ | d ____ | b ____ |
| 6. | b ____ | c ____ | d ____ | a ____ |
| 7. | c ____ | d ____ | b ____ | a ____ |
| 8. | a ____ | d ____ | b ____ | c ____ |
| 9. | c ____ | d ____ | b ____ | a ____ |
| 10. | c ____ | a ____ | d ____ | b ____ |
| 11. | a ____ | d ____ | b ____ | c ____ |
| 12. | b ____ | a ____ | c ____ | d ____ |
| 13. | a ____ | c ____ | d ____ | b ____ |
| 14. | b ____ | a ____ | d ____ | c ____ |
| 15. | c ____ | a ____ | d ____ | b ____ |
| 16. | a ____ | b ____ | d ____ | c ____ |
| 17. | d ____ | c ____ | a ____ | b ____ |
| 18. | c ____ | d ____ | b ____ | a ____ |
| 19. | a ____ | b ____ | c ____ | d ____ |
| 20. | d ____ | b ____ | c ____ | a ____ |
| **Total** | ____ | ____ | ____ | ____ |
|  | Collaborator | Innovator | Producer | Integrator |

own learning path, you can help others do the same. By moving beyond a narrow specialist or transactional mind-set and learning to cope with the challenges of transformational change, you can become the kind of managerial mentor your organization needs to compete successfully in a turbulent marketplace.

By becoming proficient in each role competency area, you will have the flexibility to apply different combinations of skills in various change situations. Depending on the nature of the change, what might work in one situation could prove counterproductive in another. For that reason, you must know what mix of managerial skills is required to deal with specific situations and have the ability to apply those skills in the right mix. Like many experienced managers, you may have shown a strong preference on the Learning Leader Role Preference Inventory for the transactional roles of Producer and Integrator. Hierarchical organizations have long emphasized and valued these roles more than the transformational roles of Collaborator and Innovator. Now and in the future, you will need to actively promote self-directed learning and build collaborative teams of people who share a common working vision. To do that, you must become a proficient Collaborator and Innovator. You must also be a competent Producer and Integrator. Many innovations fail because their creators do not realign operating systems, and many empowerment efforts fail because they are not focused on critical business issues. To be an effective managerial mentor, you must have the flexibility to utilize all four roles and competencies as situations warrant.

PART TWO | **BECOMING A LEARNING LEADER**

CHAPTERS FOUR THROUGH SEVEN articulate the four roles of the new managerial mentor. Each chapter has a similar format, beginning with an overview of the role under discussion and followed by a detailed description of each of three learning leader competencies associated with that particular role.

Case illustrations of managers demonstrating the competencies associated with each role are included to help managers see how to apply them on the job. A personal assessment tool is provided to assess individual competency levels in the four roles, together with a series of questions for competency development planning. Each chapter concludes with a recap of an individual's overall strengths and development needs in each of the four managerial mentoring roles, with suggested learning activities for improving individual performance as a Collaborator, Innovator, Producer, and Integrator.

CHAPTER FOUR

# The Learning Leader as Collaborator

IN THE COLLABORATOR ROLE, the managerial mentor is committed to expanding people's capacity for new learning and growth through relationship. The purpose is to build meaningful connections to help people identify what is important to them in their work and provide them with the personal support they need to become self-directed learners.

In the Collaborator role, the concern is with managing emotions in the workplace. Since Taylorism and the era of scientific management, the emotional side of work has been downplayed. For many years, human relations experts have promoted techniques for helping people get along, but the focus has been on creating harmony and cooperation more than on understanding the emotional side of work. Until recently, people have generally been expected to keep their feelings and emotions out of the workplace.

With the advent of the downsizing era, things changed. Disenchanted loyalists, angered by the violation of the

THE NEW MANAGERIAL MENTOR

traditional psychological contract, found themselves out on the street or struggling to cope with ever-increasing work-loads. Organizations, realizing that they needed to do something to reenergize people, embraced the notion of empowerment. Unfortunately, as is often the case with management fads, the empowerment movement soon foundered because while its organizational sponsors bought into the concept, traditional control mechanisms remained. Thus, meaningful participation became more rhetoric than reality.

By the mid-nineties, people at all organizational levels, but especially traditional managers and professionals, were outspoken in their disenchantment with the excessive demands of restructured workplaces. The fact that organizations continued to hastily implement wide-sweeping change initiatives—such as total quality management (TQM) and reengineering—only served to increase people's cynicism. Finally, organizations began to realize that in order to rebuild trust and commitment, they would have to deal with the human spirit.

As organizations tried to create working environments that would help people begin to feel a renewed sense of purpose, it became evident that managers had a new role to play. As point people at the boundary between the front lines and top management, managers were uniquely positioned to communicate the renewal message to the people whose actions would ultimately affect the organization's success. Getting that message across, however, meant that managers first had to deal with the emotional impact of downsizing.

In his recent book *Executive EQ*, organizational consultant Robert Cooper (1996) writes about the importance of *emotional intelligence*, which he defines as "the ability to sense, understand, and effectively apply the power and acumen of emotions as a source of human energy, information, connection and influence" (p. xiii). In his description of the importance of the combined intelligence of the heart and the head, Cooper makes a strong case for bringing emotions into the workplace. Thanks to the work of Cooper and others, organizations are finally beginning to understand that rebuilding trust and commitment calls for more than motivational speakers and videos from the CEO.

## The Facilitating Competency

Bookstore business shelves are full of "how-to communicate" books, and thousands of managers regularly attend workshops on the subject. The emphasis is typically on tools and techniques rather than on communicating as a way of developing authentic relationships and helping people find renewed meaning and purpose in their work. In Facilitating, managerial mentors use process wisdom to help people experience and deal with change in real time; they use their accumulated wisdom and experience in the service of others as both observers and participants in the process. Facilitating managerial mentors help individuals and teams learn how to accomplish their assigned tasks and work together more effectively.

The success of twenty-first-century organizations will depend in part on managers' ability to develop authentic relationships by using the basic Facilitating competency of empathic listening and dialogue. The acquisition of this competency will enable managerial mentors to move beyond traditional transactional relationships and act as transformational learning leaders.

Developing Facilitating competency calls for what Cooper (1996) calls *authentic presence,* a prime component of emotional intelligence. As a managerial mentor, authentic presence enables you to bring the best of yourself into listening and dialogue. Cooper (p. 68) distinguishes between the common meaning of "speech as words projected out, directed at others" and dialogue, where "you are actually inviting the other person to come inside your world, into your mind and heart." His point is that the most inspirational managers are those who are able to communicate from the heart as well as the head. The purpose of dialogue is to create shared meaning between people. That is unlikely to happen in the absence of emotional expression.

For decades, managers have been taught the technique of active listening. When psychologist Carl Rogers (1961) first coined the term *active listening*, he was referring more to values than to technique. Rogers believed very strongly in what he called *unconditional positive regard*, by which he meant nonjudgmental attentiveness to others' feelings. Rogers felt that people who actively listen are more effective because others trust them and want to work with them. He saw listening as empowering because it enables people to learn how to solve their own problems. He believed that listening is important because everyone has something worthwhile to say.

## Facilitating in Practice

As the result of a major downsizing and reorganization, Marilyn Weller was assigned the position of advertising and circulation manager for a major metropolitan newspaper. Prior to the downsizing, advertising and circulation were separate departments comprising fifteen and thirty-two people, respectively. Now the merged department numbered thirty-three, with eight advertising and twenty-five circulation staff. The former manager of the circulation unit, forty-four-year-old Marilyn had been with the newspaper for fifteen years. She had a reputation as a savvy sales producer, successfully increasing circulation when other papers were losing business. The advertising staff were clearly unhappy about the merger with circulation. They saw themselves as creative professionals and did not like being lumped with people they viewed as salesclerks. They were even angrier about the fact that their department had lost nearly half its staff while circulation had lost proportionately fewer people.

After the merger, Marilyn held several group meetings to try to sell everyone on the reorganization plan. While the circulation staff bought in, the advertising people acted passively aggressive and refused to accept the change. The more Marilyn tried to sell them on the idea, the more they resisted. Realizing that there was no way that she could persuade the advertising staff to buy in, Marilyn tried to put herself in their shoes to better understand why they felt so angry. Once she was able to empathize with their feelings of loss and diminished self-esteem, she decided that her best tactic would be to deal directly with their anger. Working through the emotional issues might be the only way to move forward.

In several painful but productive sessions, Marilyn helped the staff understand the stages of change and what they needed to do to move through them. She encouraged the circulation people to actively support their new colleagues and worked with the entire group to develop a transition process. Once the advertising staff were able to vent their anger, they were better able to participate in the planning process. The transition did not always go smoothly, but by continuing to meet with the group on a regular basis to assess progress and redefine roles and responsibilities, Marilyn was able to get everyone on board and focus on the future.

Marilyn Weller's experience is a good example of Facilitating in action. She realized that while the expression of emotion was not the norm in the organization, people were stuck in their anger and no amount of wheedling and cajoling would move them out of it. Her initial reaction of trying to make it go away through rational persuasion was a typical managerial reaction. It was not until she was able to realize that emotions in the workplace are a normal part of business life, especially in transitional times, that she was able to successfully deal with the issue.

## Assessing Your Facilitating Competency

Listening is critical to developing your Facilitating competency. It is probably the most important thing you can do to build positive working relationships. Attending a seminar on active listening may give you some useful listening techniques, but it will not turn you into a good listener. Deep listening means seeing, watching, feeling, and caring about the speaker. While most of us are born with the physical ability to hear, hearing is not synonymous with listening. Listening is a learned skill.

There are three levels of listening, and most people listen at all three levels during the typical work day. The first level is the most superficial and involves tuning in and out on what is being said. Often, the listener has her mind on other things and is not really attending to the speaker. At the second level, the listener is hearing the words but is listening more for content than feeling and is not really involved in the conversation. At this level, it is very easy to misinterpret

## EXERCISE 2: **LISTENING SKILLS CHECKLIST**

| Do You | Yes | No |
|---|---|---|
| 1. Let the speaker express anger at you without getting defensive? | ___ | ___ |
| 2. Try to hear what is being said, even when you're not really interested? | ___ | ___ |
| 3. Believe that you can learn something from everyone you meet? | ___ | ___ |
| 4. Avoid thinking about how to refute what someone is saying while they're still talking? | ___ | ___ |
| 5. Take into consideration the temperament of the person you're listening to? | ___ | ___ |
| 6. Reiterate what you heard to make sure that you understand what was said? | ___ | ___ |
| 7. Avoid interrupting the speaker before he or she has finished talking? | ___ | ___ |

what is being communicated. The third listening level is what Rogers (1961) calls active, or empathic, listening. This is what Marilyn Weller did when she put herself in the shoes of her angry advertising staff. In empathic listening, the listener does not judge what is being said but focuses on trying to understand things from the speaker's point of view. Deep listening involves attention to nonverbal cues and underlying feelings. Learning how to listen with empathy is an important part of Facilitating. Exercise 2 (above and on page 54) will help you assess your current listening habits and pinpoint the areas where you need to improve your listening skills.

## EXERCISE 2: **LISTENING SKILLS CHECKLIST** (cont'd)

| Do You | Yes | No |
|---|---|---|
| 8. Try to keep from listening selectively to hear only what you want to hear? | ___ | ___ |
| 9. Listen for nonverbal and emotional tone cues as well as the words spoken? | ___ | ___ |
| 10. Paraphrase the feelings underlying the words being spoken? | ___ | ___ |
| 11. Look at the person while he or she is talking? | ___ | ___ |
| 12. Listen to the other person's views even though you may disagree? | ___ | ___ |
| 13. Keep a few notes to help you remember later what the person said? | ___ | ___ |
| 14. Know what words or phrases press your "hot button" when you hear them? | ___ | ___ |
| 15. Think about how the other person might react to what you are saying? | ___ | ___ |

If you have more than a few No responses, you need to do some serious work on improving your listening skills. Even if you have mostly Yes responses, you can probably enhance your empathic listening ability. Because we do not always see ourselves the way others see us, you may wish to ask one or more people you work closely with and trust to assess you on these same questions. You can then use these assessment data to outline some listening improvement steps to enhance your Facilitating skills.

## EXERCISE 3: **LISTENING SKILLS IMPROVEMENT STEPS**

1. Based on your listening assessment data, what specific behaviors do you need to work on to improve your listening skills?

2. In what specific situations at work might practicing more empathic listening improve your communications with others?

3. Think of someone at work you have difficulty listening to, and describe what it is about their behavior that turns you off. What can you do to either modify your own reaction or help that person approach you differently?

4. Who is a trusted person at work or away from work with whom you can practice your listening improvement steps and get feedback on your progress?

5. How can improved listening skills enhance your ability to accomplish important work goals?

## Developing Your Facilitating Competency

Exercise 3 provides a series of questions to help you improve your listening skills. Based on your responses to Exercise 2 and your feedback from others, you can identify specific listening improvement steps.

## The Coaching Competency

The second Collaborator competency, Coaching, is one of the most important managerial mentoring tasks. Over the years, managerial coaching has been a popular topic in the business press. Twenty years ago, Ferdinand Fournies published *Coaching for Improved Work Performance* (1987, rev. ed.), a behavior change approach to performance improvement. Since that time, many sports figures have published motivational books on coaching, such as Vince Lombardi's (1995) *Coaching for Teamwork: Winning Concepts for Business in the Twenty-First Century*. The idea of the "personal coach" is a recent trend, and people are hiring coaches to advise them on all aspects of their lives. One of the more promising new approaches is the concept of coaching as a co-learning experience for both managers and the people they coach. Co-learning is a good description of the learning leader Coaching competency.

In coaching others, managerial mentors initiate and actively participate in hands-on learning. They are not mentors in the traditional sense of offering career advice and advocacy. Rather, they are learning guides who use their knowledge and experience to accompany people in the co-learning process. In *The Leadership Engine*, Noel Tichy (1997) talks about the fact that great leaders are great teachers because they are extraordinary learners. They analyze their experiences, draw lessons from them, and continually refine their views as they acquire new knowledge and experience. Managerial mentors use that knowledge and experience to help others learn.

Participating in co-learning experiences can be a powerful catalyst for managerial mentors, especially corporate survivors who may question the value of their work and their ability to make a meaningful contribution. Noer (1993) and others have described how corporate survivors tend to get entrenched in the past and hold on to learning strategies that have lost their currency. As a result, they do not learn the new skills needed to thrive in transitional times.

In thinking about the role of the new managerial mentor, it is useful to recall the origins in Greek mythology of the word *mentor*. Mentor was the name of a teacher asked by Odysseus to watch over his son Telemachus during Odysseus's long voyage. Mentor guided and nurtured the boy until Odysseus's return many years later.

Chungliang Al Huang and Jerry Lynch (1995), authors of *Mentoring*, describe an even earlier model of mentoring demonstrated in the succession practices of three Chinese kings between 2333 and 2177 B.C. These ancient mentors resembled our new managerial mentors in that their focus was on sharing learning and wisdom more than on guiding the development of another. The authors of this book build their mentoring model on the Taoist teachings of self-reflection, simplicity, openness to others, and personal sharing. Mentoring, in their view, is a process of shared learning and growth in which both parties benefit from mutual interaction and support. The focus is less on teaching and more on learning how to learn together. Psychologist Carl Rogers (1961) claimed that things of little importance can be taught, but things of real significance can only be learned.

In the Coaching competency, managerial mentors act neither as pseudo-therapists nor as behavior modification specialists. Rather, they engage in what coaching consultant Kendall Murphy (1995) calls *generative coaching*. As a former district manager for Pacific Bell, Murphy came to the realization that listening and asking questions worked better than traditional command-and-control practices. Murphy defines generative coaching as "a way of understanding people in their wholeness, followed by conversations (language) and actions (practices) consistent with that understanding" (p. 202). He strongly believes that generative coaching is essential to the creation of a true learning organization.

Learning organization proponents and practitioners tend to agree that real learning comes from the hearts and minds of individuals, not from top-down attempts to engineer organizational learning. In the Coaching competency, managerial mentors facilitate individual growth that contributes to a thirst for continual learning, which eventually spreads from individuals to teams and to entire organizations.

Coaching happens in conversations, and as a managerial mentor, you must create a willingness on the part of people to collaborate with you in that process. By showing that you really care about people's development, you help them develop the motivation and skills to accomplish the work that needs to get done now and in the future. The fact that Coaching conversations are about performance does not mean that they focus only on tasks and objectives. Coaching can be about anything that helps the person learn and grow on the job, such as feedback on interpersonal skills, networking know-how, or performance improvement needs. Anything that has a present or future impact on a person's performance is a suitable coaching topic. Successful coaching comes from mutual information sharing and the trust, candor, and learning that comes from that collaborative process.

## Coaching in Practice

The following excerpt is from a Coaching conversation between a managerial mentor and a staff member, a downsizing survivor in a large consulting firm that markets corporate training programs.

**Survivor:** Since the last downsizing, I've been putting more and more pressure on my people to get out there and sell, sell, sell. I tell them that if we don't increase the numbers soon, we'll all be out on the street.

**Coach:** You say you think increasing sales is your best strategy. Tell me how you got there. What led you to that conclusion?

**Survivor:** Well, that's what has always worked for us in the past, and as far as I can tell it's still the best strategy if we just work harder. What I need to do is ride herd until we get the numbers up.

**Coach:** So your approach now is to push people harder and remind them that if they don't produce, everyone's going to lose. Do you have any thoughts about why that approach doesn't seem to be working?

**Survivor:** Yes, I guess they see me as a hard-nosed SOB who is putting the onus on them to get the job done. Actually, that's not the case, but I can't let them think that I don't have things under control. Actually, I don't have a clue about what to do to help us survive.

**Coach:** You say that while you are aware that people think you're putting an unfair burden on them, you can't let them think that you don't have all the answers. Can you think of a possible way that you might be able to get the message across that you really are concerned about the impact on them, but that under the circumstances you just don't see any alternative?

**Survivor:** Well, some of them have been complaining about the fact that we're putting all of our energies into selling our established training line—which has been phenomenally successful over the years—instead of going out in the marketplace asking people about their emerging needs and finding out if they want something new and different, and what we can do to deliver it.

**Coach:** What's your feeling about that?

**Survivor:** Well, it's a fine idea over the long haul, but it won't bring in the dollars and save us now.

**Coach:** Is it really an either-or decision? Isn't there some way you and your team could do both?

**Survivor:** Perhaps, but I don't want them thinking that I don't know what I'm doing. Okay, it might not hurt to discuss the question. Maybe it's a bit unfair on my part to assume that the only reason they're suggesting this is because it's a nice excuse for not bringing in new business.

**Coach:** So then one thing you might do is get your team together and open up a dialogue about the situation. By asking them questions and listening to what they have to say, they might feel that you understand how tough it is on everyone, and you might get some good customer data. After all, they're the ones out there talking to the people.

Notice how the coach draws out the person she is coaching, helping him see that his tactic might not be the best one for the situation. At the point when he is willing to consider the possibility that there might be another alternative, the coach offers a suggestion in a nonthreatening way.

## Assessing Your Coaching Competency

In developing your Coaching competency, you will replace management-by-control with management-by-commitment. You will be actively involved with your direct reports, and your contacts will be developmentally oriented. The emphasis will be on learning and stimulating people to develop new competencies. Corrective coaching will still be part of the process, but your overall focus will be more developmental in nature.

The Coaching competency of the learning leader cuts across all four managerial mentoring roles, such as the Innovator role of stimulating creative thinking by sharing new ideas with people, or the Producer role of helping people set challenging performance targets. Exercise 4 on pages 61—62 will help you assess your current level of Coaching competency and provide you with a basis for personal development planning.

## EXERCISE 4: **COACHING PRACTICES CHECKLIST**

| Do You | Yes | No |
|---|---|---|
| 1. Encourage people to focus on the most important parts of the job? | ___ | ___ |
| 2. Regularly share your own knowledge and expertise with people? | ___ | ___ |
| 3. Give people regular feedback on their demonstrated strengths? | ___ | ___ |
| 4. Actively encourage people to seek out new challenges? | ___ | ___ |
| 5. Make a personal effort to support people who are having job problems? | ___ | ___ |
| 6. Try to help people see the importance of the work they are doing? | ___ | ___ |
| 7. Actively encourage people to look for creative solutions to problems? | ___ | ___ |
| 8. Inspire people to want to go the extra mile in their work? | ___ | ___ |
| 9. Try to encourage people to learn from their failures? | ___ | ___ |
| 10. Make an effort to avoid the tendency to micromanage? | ___ | ___ |
| 11. Try to maintain friendly and informal relationships with people? | ___ | ___ |
| 12. Regularly offer people new training and development opportunities? | ___ | ___ |

## EXERCISE 4: **COACHING PRACTICES CHECKLIST**
(cont'd)

| Do You | Yes | No |
| --- | --- | --- |
| 13. Keep people informed about top management plans and strategies? | ____ | ____ |
| 14. Try to keep people motivated in difficult and stressful times? | ____ | ____ |
| 15. Make a demonstrable effort to lead by example? | ____ | ____ |

## Developing Your Coaching Competency

Even if you answer Yes to quite a few of the questions in the preceding instrument, the chances are that you still need to think about ways in which to enhance your overall Coaching competency. There is probably not a more important area of learning for you as a managerial mentor. Your challenge is to learn how to get each individual on your team committed to the group's mission and goals. The questions in Exercise 5 will help you think about your Coaching competency development needs.

## The Dialoguing Competency

Dialoguing is the third Collaborator competency. Dialoguing is sorely needed in the world today. In an article in *Organizational Dynamics*, William Isaacs (1993) refers to former Israeli Foreign Minister Abba Eban's observation about leaders at the G7 Summit in 1993 that, while they represented a

## EXERCISE 5: **COACHING COMPETENCY DEVELOPMENT STEPS**

1. What do you see as some of your current Coaching strengths, and what can you do to enhance them?

2. What specific Coaching practices do you need to work on to improve your overall competency in this area?

3. What kinds of formal or informal learning experiences might help you improve your Coaching competency?

4. Who is someone that you consider to be successful at Coaching and what does he or she do that leads you to that conclusion?

5. How will improving your Coaching competency directly contribute to the achievement of your performance goals?

THE NEW MANAGERIAL MENTOR

tremendous concentration of international power, their efforts did not seem to produce much because they thought individually rather than collectively. Isaacs writes that given the complex, interdependent, and potentially catastrophic nature of political and institutional problems today, people must develop their capacity for collaborative thinking and coordinated action. Isaacs and his colleagues at the Dialogue Project at M.I.T. are working with diverse organizations on an emerging discipline of dialogue that has great potential to facilitate learning in organizations. Dialogue transforms the quality of normal conversation and the thinking that goes into it. While we typically think of coordinated action as a product of shared agreement and joint action planning, dialogue does not assume that coordinated action always depends upon rational planning.

Dialogue is different from consensus building. The latter is a rational process in which people try to limit options and settle on a view that everyone can live with. The problem with consensus is that even though people may express agreement on an issue, the different thinking patterns that caused their initial disagreement remain unchanged; that is, there is no opportunity to explore or alter the underlying patterns of meaning. In dialogue, people learn how to think together by surfacing their fundamental assumptions and developing insight into how they arose.

The fact that organizations today exist in a world of ever-increasing complexity means that no one individual is capable of dealing with the myriad problems that require creative and timely solutions. Yet organizations find it very difficult to get people to dialogue and learn together. Teams polarize around familiar positions, and people are unwilling to raise difficult or controversial issues. As a result, the learning that does occur is often dysfunctional and tends to perpetuate the status quo. When breakthrough solutions are created, organizations are apt to get stuck in the new pattern and fail to see the need for ongoing renewal as a way of being.

Another major barrier to collaborative learning is the tendency for people to think as specialists in a particular field and, as such, to defend a narrow point of view. By developing the Dialoguing competency, managerial mentors can help people learn how to converse in nondefensive ways to build creative collaborations. In spite of decades of team building, true collaborations are still rare because people have not learned how to engage in authentic dialogue. They remain locked in defensive routines and are reluctant to challenge the status quo, fearing that if they raise controversial issues or disagree with the group, they will be labeled poor team players.

Nondefensive listening, discussed earlier in the chapter, is a key factor in creating effective dialogue. Instead of listening, the norm in many organizations is to look for holes in another person's point of view, especially when trying to impress a boss. Therefore, it is especially important for managerial mentors as learning leaders to take an active role in helping make dialogue the new norm in practice.

## Dialoguing in Practice

Dialogue was the primary teaching method employed by Socrates in ancient Greece. It was a kind of conversation that he taught by asking students a series of ongoing questions to challenge their underlying assumptions and beliefs. Dialogue was also the process used by the citizens of Athens to resolve differences. When there was a problem, they would meet in the marketplace and hold a dialogue for as long as it took to arrive at a collective insight. Gradually, however, the busy Athenians began to replace dialogue with debate and employed advocates to represent their respective views. Debate, rather than dialogue, has emerged over the years as the primary model for resolving differences between groups. Debate, as practiced in modern democracies, is about defending a position and winning an argument; dialogue is about suspending judgment and listening with an open mind. It is based on the assumption that by sharing points of view and exploring new possibilities we can learn from difference and create a common wisdom.

An important step at the outset of the dialoguing process is the creation of a "container" to help people break out of the traditional problem-solving mode and be prepared to listen to each other in a nonjudgmental way. The following example portrays a dialogue session involving representatives from two hospitals in a small city in the Southwest and the hospitals' out-of-state owner. Participants attended a dinner party the night before the first session to share thoughts and feelings about readings from great thinkers and writers of the twentieth century, which they had received earlier. Over dinner, participants were able to engage in lively conversation and get to know one other in ways that otherwise might not have been possible.

The dialogue session came about because of escalating tensions between the local hospitals and their out-of-state owner. The hospitals, all in financial difficulty, had been acquired several months earlier by a large out-of-state managed-care corporation. The general agreement at the time of purchase was that the corporate owner would permit the hospitals to retain operational autonomy as long as they collaborated to deliver more cost-effective health care services to the community and make the corporation's investment profitable. In the ensuing months, the corporate owner became increasingly frustrated over the apparent lack of progress in cost management and started to get more actively involved in day-to-day operations. This angered everyone, especially the hospitals' physicians, who already perceived their administrators as inept bureaucrats.

Attending the dialogue session were the two hospital administrators and their managers, key physicians, executives representing the corporate owner, and interested parties from the local community. At the outset, facilitators worked with the group to understand the ground rules of dialogue, such as nonjudgmental listening, questioning of assumptions, refraining from speech making, and so on. Given their conflicting interests, the escalating tensions, and the potential impact on the community, it was particularly important for participants to take the time to explore in depth rather than engage in debate or try to come up with a "right" solution.

After the first session, it became clear to the participants that in light of their diverse perspectives and limited experience in collaborative conversation, developing a true spirit of inquiry would require real commitment and considerable time. Each party found it difficult to acknowledge that other parties had legitimate concerns. The local health care professionals were uniformly distrustful of what they perceived as the "back East" mind-set of the corporate owner. The physicians were not skilled communicators and were aggressively vocal about their right to make independent decisions. The hospital administrators felt caught in the middle and were concerned that nobody seemed to understand the complexities of trying to contain costs in a system in chaos. The community representatives felt that nobody really cared about the interests of health care consumers, and that they would be the ultimate losers.

By following the basic ground rules of dialogue, the participants gradually developed the ability to listen to conflicting views, test underlying assumptions, and explore new models for profitably providing quality health care to the community. As trust increased among participants, there was less polarization and more learning. While they acknowledged that there would always be value differences between patient-care professionals and bottom-line managers, they used the creative tension generated by these differences as a source of productive dialogue. The most important outcome of the dialogue experience was that formerly polarized parties were able to shift the focus from their own self-interests to how to develop a collaborative model to best meet the health care needs of the community.

## Assessing Your Dialoguing Competency

Since most of us have been trained to debate rather than to dialogue, you will probably need to develop a new approach to conversation and relationship building. The questions in Exercise 6 will give you insight into how you currently approach these processes. For each item, select either alternative **a** or alternative **b**.

If you chose the **a** response for most of the items, your behavior is more like that of a debater than a dialoguer. That would be understandable given that in most organizations debate is still the common way to resolve disagreements and arrive at decisions. Dialogue, however, can be a powerful force for organizational transformation. If organizations truly value innovation, dialogue is an excellent vehicle for making it happen.

## EXERCISE 6: **ASSESSING YOUR DIALOGUING COMPETENCY**

1.  When you are preparing to talk about a controversial issue are you more apt to:
    a. know what you think and focus on the arguments you will need to make
    b. have an idea about what you think but go in wanting to hear what others think

2.  In conversing with others, are you more interested in
    a. coming up with timely answers
    b. asking questions to explore issues in-depth

3.  Is it more valuable to you to come out of a conversation with
    a. a clear picture of which argument made the most sense
    b. a shared understanding of different points of view

4.  On controversial issues, do you think that most of the time
    a. somebody is right and somebody is wrong
    b. every point of view has some validity

5.  In listening to a point of view that is different from yours, are you more apt to
    a. try to win the other person over to your point of view
    b. seek out information as to how the other person came to that view

6.  In participating in a controversial conversation, are you more comfortable
    a. defending your position
    b. exploring new possibilities

## Developing Your Dialoguing Competency

The best way to develop your Dialoguing competency is to participate in a dialogue group. Today, such sessions are being run in companies, schools, and community organizations, and the practice is spreading. In a dialogue group, usually composed of ten to twenty people, participants sit in a circle and make a commitment to being fully present throughout the session; that is, they are willing to be honest, open, and nonjudgmental. Everyone is responsible for holding the group's energy and maintaining a spirit of inquiry. Some dialogue groups focus on a specific topic, others are open and nondirected, and still others set a vague theme but let the conversation flow freely.

Successful participation in a dialogue session requires a high degree of self-awareness. In *The Fifth Discipline Handbook*, Senge, Roberts, Ross, Smith, and Kleiner (1994) offer an exercise called Moments of Awareness that you can use to develop your Dialoguing competency. It involves asking yourself a series of self-reflective questions that can be especially helpful in volatile or argumentative situations. The following example shows how this process was helpful in defusing a confrontation during a diversity training session when the facilitator, an African American female, accused by a white male manager of advocating reverse discrimination, blew up at her accuser. Here is how the facilitator used the process, the steps of which are italicized:

1. *What is happening?* "In spite of everything I've said all day about equal opportunity not involving special preference, this guy has refused to listen and now he's hit my hot button."

2. *What are you doing?* "I'm in an argument with him."

3. *What are you feeling?* "Plenty angry."

4. *What are you thinking?* "That this guy is a racist pig who has been sitting waiting for a chance to go at me."

5. *How are you breathing?* "Very shallow to try to get myself under control."

6. *What do you want for yourself?* "I don't want to get into it with this jerk in front of the entire group. There is a creep like this in every session and nothing works with them. His redneck mentality makes these sessions incredibly difficult, and I can't figure out how to get through to people like him. Now I've played right into his hands by letting him get to me."

7. *What are you doing to prevent yourself from getting what you want?* "I'm playing right into his hands by getting so upset. I need to calm down and tell him that I apologize for blowing up at him and would like to hear more about why he assumes that equal opportunity is reverse discrimination."

8. *Take a deep breath and move on.* By taking a "time out" to reflect on her feelings, the facilitator was able to defuse her anger and choose another way to deal with the situation. And by afterward sharing with the group how she had dealt with the incident, she provided a live demonstration of the value of the process.

You can practice this exercise in any situation in which you feel anxious, upset, or angry. The ability to self-reflect is critical to the development of your Dialoguing competency, and you will find it useful in both personal and professional interactions.

## The Collaborator in Action

Jonathan Rivers was recently appointed president of Eastern Employee Assistance Services, a fast-growing organization that provides employee counseling and consulting services to companies throughout New England. At age forty-four, Jonathan has more than twenty years of management experience in both the corporate and social sectors. In his most recent position as director of wellness for a medium-sized insurance company, Jonathan was responsible for creating and managing both that organization's in-house wellness programs and its health promotion consulting services for policyholders. Prior to that, he served as a human resource manager for a small manufacturer. With both an M.B.A. and an M.S.W., Jonathan is well qualified to help Eastern move forward.

Over the last two years, Eastern has endured many traumatic changes. As a result, people are discouraged and morale is low. Jonathan was hired to replace the most recent president, who was fired after less than a year on the job. The organization's founding president was killed two years ago in a plane crash. After his death, the board of directors decided to wait a while before finding a replacement, and a vice president was appointed to serve on an interim basis while the board decided what to do. The vice president, a twenty-eight-year-old female M.S.W. with no prior management experience, tried to hold things together, but with little support from the board she soon became the scapegoat for the anger and frustration associated with the loss of the founder. When the board made the decision to hire a new president, she applied for the job but was rejected and soon thereafter left the organization.

The board, realizing that there was no way they could replace the charismatic founder, who had been revered by the staff, decided to look for a strong, directive leader who would help the organization get moving again. The growth of the business continued to explode, particularly in substance abuse training, and new client companies were coming to Eastern on a regular basis. The staff of twenty-eight struggled to meet the increased business demands, but without a clear sense of purpose and direction and with too much work, service quality started to decline.

The board decided to act and appointed a new president, a retired naval officer with an impressive track record at the Pentagon. He seemed like the ideal candidate to get the staff back on track, but his authoritarian management style soon alienated both the staff and the board, and things went even further downhill. The board finally decided to terminate his services and started a new search.

When Jonathan Rivers came on board, his first step was to call a special session of the staff to introduce himself, give the staff an opportunity to vent their frustrations, talk about his entry-level agenda, and respond to their questions.

Jonathan spent considerable time providing the staff with an overview of his entry-level agenda. He said that he would be meeting individually with each staff member over the next few weeks to get their input on how they would like to see things go forward and what they wanted in the way of support and staff development. He added that he would also be meeting with each of the program units—counseling, consulting services, and so forth—to familiarize himself with their needs and priorities. He announced that he would establish a business transition team composed of the heads of each of the program units plus two members to be chosen by the staff at large. While the overall purpose of this group would be to provide him with strategic business input, he added that he expected the business transition team to take responsibility for spelling out their specific activities.

When Jonathan opened up the session for questions, he received the full brunt of the staff's frustrations. He listened without comment and listed each concern on a flip chart. At the end of an exhausting but exhilarating session, he announced that he would review their expressed concerns and get back to them with his thoughts within three weeks. Over the next few weeks, Jonathan not only met with individual staff members and the program units as promised, he made himself visible and available around the organization.

At the end of three weeks, Jonathan called another staff session. He shared his responses to the staff's expressed concerns and told them about a few changes that he would initiate immediately. He said he thought that many of the issues they had raised might best be addressed through staff dialogue. He offered specific suggestions about how they could set up such a process, and the staff responded positively to the idea. He then turned the meeting over to the business transition team, who reported on their progress and requested feedback on their proposed action plan. Several staff members offered suggestions, and the overall plan was well received.

Jonathan thanked everyone for their hard work and support and told them that his next step would be to share the results of their efforts with the board. He reiterated how excited he was about the future of the organization and how pleased he was to be working there.

## Becoming an Effective Collaborator

In the case you just read, Jonathan Rivers demonstrated a number of positive characteristics of the new managerial

## EXERCISE 7: **DEVELOPING YOUR COLLABORATOR ROLE**

........................................................................................................

1. Given the situation at the time he was hired, what did the former president do or not do that contributed to his early termination? What could he have done differently?

2. What do you think about Jonathan's decision to call a staff session so soon after his arrival? What would you have done? Why?

........................................................................................................

mentor. As you focus on the questions in Exercise 7 (above and on page 76), think about the ways in which Jonathan demonstrated the three Collaborator competencies—Facilitating, Coaching, and Dialoguing—and what the case says to you about your own strengths and development needs in each of these three competency areas.

The Collaborator's overarching purpose is to build learning partnerships that motivate each member of the organization to want to reach his or her full potential and contribute to the success of the organization. For an organization to maintain a long-term competitive advantage, each individual must be fully committed to an exciting vision of the organization's future. That is the role of the managerial mentor as Innovator, to be discussed in the next chapter.

## EXERCISE 7: **DEVELOPING YOUR COLLABORATOR ROLE** (cont'd)

3. What did Jonathan do that demonstrated the Facilitating competency? The Coaching competency? The Dialoguing competency?

4. Do you agree or disagree with Jonathan's decision to put together a business transition team? Why?

5. How would you have approached the job if you had been hired as president? How does your approach relate to your scores on the Learning Leader Role Preference Inventory?

6. Which of the three Collaborator competencies—Facilitating, Coaching, or Dialoguing—do you need to focus on to enhance your effectiveness in the Collaborator role?

7. What specific learning activities, on or off the job, might you undertake to become a more competent collaborator?

CHAPTER FIVE

# The Learning Leader as Innovator

THE SECOND ROLE OF the managerial mentor is that of Innovator. The Innovator helps people learn how to survive and thrive in times of change. Organizations today have the potential to become places in which a sense of community and a commitment to learning is the cultural norm. In his introduction to *The Organization of the Future*, Peter Drucker (1997) says: "Command and control is being replaced by or intermixed with all kinds of relationships: alliances, joint ventures, minority participations, partnerships, know-how, and marketing agreements. . . . These relationships have to be based on a common understanding of objectives, policies, and strategies; on teamwork; and on persuasion—or they do not work at all" (p. 2).

In a concluding essay in the same volume, social philosopher Charles Handy (1997) writes about the emerging virtual organization, in which workplaces are no longer the tangible, visible places they used to be and people do not need to be in the same place at the same time to get things done. As a result, the leader must articulate a mission and vision and develop commitment on the part of people in diverse locations and circumstances. In the virtual organization, Handy says, power comes from relationships, not structures, and the task becomes one of finding a mission and vision that people can understand and strive to achieve in a variety of relationships. In the organization of the future, the glue that holds things together will be a clear mission, vision, and set of core principles that provide a basis for trust and commitment. Trust, in other words, will be the basis for new relationships where no one controls and no one commands.

In an era of downsizing and restructuring, it is sadly evident that many people find little or no meaning or satisfaction in their work. Many would like to retire early. Yet it is becoming increasingly clear that most people in the twenty-first century will need to work until age seventy-five in order to survive financially in a society in which people are living longer and governments are cutting back on benefits.

Much of today's work is dehumanizing, and management relationships often demean and demoralize rather than enhance and empower. This relationship problem is not limited to entry-level or low-skill service jobs; it is also true for managerial and professional jobs. Any organization that wants to thrive in the next century must find a way to help its members find renewed meaning and purpose in their work.

Peter Senge (1990b) writes that creating a shared vision is central to all else that an organization does. As a managerial mentor, you cannot create a vision and expect people passively to follow your lead. You may create a working vision, but as a learning leader you will then dialogue with others to develop a shared vision. In that way, people will learn how to take responsibility for their own work outcomes and become more personally accountable.

Self-responsibility assumes that people are willing and able to provide each other with what was formerly provided by top-down leadership. Mutual accountability is what will hold things together in the future. While some form of hierarchy will endure, leadership will be shared and the role of the managerial mentor will be to engage people in learning and leading. Mentors will not be just teachers and role models, they will be convenors; they will not be just visionary leaders, they will be integrators of diverse visions.

In *Real Change Leaders*, Katzenbach and the RCL Team (1995) describe a new breed of change leader. Their research led them to conclude that middle managers, whom they call *real change leaders*, or RCLs, possess a unique ability to create high-performing organizations by changing the skills and behavior of many people. These authors refer to RCLs as fundamentalists because of their belief, like early management theorists, that a successful business is both a social and an economic institution and must be led accordingly. RCLs believe in self-governance and joint accountability for the creation of new opportunities through open dialogue and conflict resolution. This process, they believe, will ensure the airing of diverse perspectives and the making of informed decisions.

One of the most informative parts of *Real Change Leaders*, and one that has special relevance for the managerial mentor as Innovator, is its concept of the working vision. Realizing that many visions are the outcome of senior management wordsmithing at corporate retreats, the authors cite the need for practical, compelling visions like John F. Kennedy's vision in 1961 to put a man on the moon by the end of the decade.

They make the point that a good vision energizes people and motivates them to commit to a cause. Since most corporate visions are highly abstract, the task of managerial mentors as Innovators, like RCLs, will be to create unit visions that serve as practical tools for managing change. These local visions can have organization wide relevance, or they can be confined to a single change project.

## The Visioning Competency

The first competency of the managerial mentor as Innovator is Visioning. The Innovator creates a working vision that paints a clear, compelling picture for everyone involved of what needs to change. Rather than some idealized future state, the Innovator focuses on current reality and strives to help people see and feel the need for change. The Innovator wants people to connect with a reality that they know rather than a utopian vision of the future. His or her assumption is that the energy for change comes from people's ability to look internally and externally to clearly see problems and potentials and threats and opportunities. The Innovator helps people create a realistic working vision of the future through a process of shared exploration of organizational issues and concerns.

The Innovator who is competent at Visioning is not synonymous with the visionary who inspires others through sheer genius. He or she is more of a creative collaborator who fosters an atmosphere that brings out the genius in others. In his case study of creative leaders, *Organizing Genius*, Warren Bennis (1997) says that in great groups there is usually one person who acts as a maestro. Bennis describes such a person as "a pragmatic dreamer . . . with an original, but attainable vision . . . able to realize his or her dream only if the others are free to do exceptional work . . . one who recruits the others by making the vision so palpable and seductive that they see it, too, and eagerly sign up" (p. 19).

Bennis thinks of such people as curators rather than creators because they use their ability to identify talented people and bring them into the fold. He cites the example of World War II scientist Robert Oppenheimer, who could not perform the specific tasks required to create the atomic bomb but was able to enlist people who could and work with them to complete the project.

In successful Visioning, a working vision is never finished; it is always subject to revision because change is not the result of one vision but of many aligned visions. Learning leaders are the ones who keep all the visions aligned. They see that new team members are given the opportunity to understand and internalize the unit's working vision. They understand that working visions are not cast in stone and must be continually revised to accommodate changes in the organization's internal and external environment. In practicing the Visioning competency, learning leaders act as maestros.

The essence of the Visioning competency is helping people learn how to think together to design and develop products and services that no one individual could imagine alone. This is easier said than done. Many books have been written on creative thinking, and organizations have spent millions of dollars on creativity training programs. Some organizations lock up innovators in think tanks; others tolerate them but view them as impractical mavericks. The end result is that while most organizations pay lip service to the importance of innovation, few know how to practice it. Such organizations have not yet learned that innovation is something that people do together.

## Visioning in Practice

One organization that successfully harnesses the creative energy of its people is IDEO Product Development, where for founder David Kelley and his colleagues, "work is play, brainstorming is a science, and the most important rule is to break the rules" (O'Brien, 1996, p. 92). With headquarters in Palo Alto, California, IDEO is one of the most influential design firms in the world. In offices around the world, it creates innovative products ranging from Levelor blinds and Crest toothpaste containers to AT&T telephones and answering machines. IDEO has no bosses or job titles; people organize into project teams that form and disband on a regular basis. While fun and freedom are the norm, IDEO's people have to produce tangible products quickly. Kelley says that brainstorming is the primary engine for innovation. IDEO's five brainstorming principles are prominently displayed for all to see: Stay focused on the topic, Encourage wild ideas, Defer judgment, Build on the ideas of others, One conversation at a time. After brainstorming sessions, project teams select the best ideas and move quickly to develop them. Kelley emphasizes the quickness factor and feels that enlightened trial and error beats careful planning. A good indication of IDEO's success is that in 1996, Steelcase, a large office furniture company, made a major investment in IDEO and named David Kelley its vice president of technical discovery and innovation.

## Assessing Your Visioning Competency

According to Peter Senge (1990b), the creation of a shared vision is central to all else that an organization does. Yet we tend not to think of our work as something that we can create because we have been educated to think more about the *hows* than the *whys* of our activities. We go about our work without thinking about our purpose or what we are trying to create.

Robert Fritz (1991), author of *Creating*, was one of the first people to make the word *vision* popular in management circles. Now he acknowledges some regret about having done so because of the way the term has been misused and trivialized. Unlike the vague and superficial vision statements that appear in corporate reports, Fritz sees vision as a living, breathing, tangible thing. It might be about an organization's overall purpose, its strategy, or its goals. The common element in all meaningful visions is that they articulate a clear picture of the desired end result we wish to achieve. Once that vision is clarified, the next step is to assess current reality and observe the discrepancy between the two. Fritz uses the term *creative tension* to describe the energy generated when people try to resolve the gap between vision and current reality. If the vision is really meaningful to people, it mobilizes them to action.

Developing your Visioning competency enables you to design a future of your own choosing and gain more control over your own destiny. Your vision is based on your belief that what you envision will be good for you, your unit, and your organization. Creating such a vision is one of your most critical roles as a learning leader because it forces you to take a stand on something you are willing to take risks for. It channels your most important values and creates a tangible picture of how you want those values lived out in your unit.

The questions in Exercise 8 on pages 84—85 will help you assess your Visioning competency.

If you already have a working vision for your unit, you can use Exercise 8 to critique that vision. Your current vision

## EXERCISE 8: **VISIONING COMPETENCY CHECKLIST**

|  | Yes | No |
|---|---|---|

1. Do the people in your unit have a clear vision of the contribution your unit will make to the goals of the organization? _____ _____

2. Do the people in your unit have a shared understanding of the kinds of values you will live by in the unit? _____ _____

3. Have the people in your unit actively participated in the creation of the unit's vision? _____ _____

4. Does everyone in your unit know who your internal customers are and how you will work with them? _____ _____

5. Does your unit's vision lend itself to the creation of the structures, policies, and practices needed to support it? _____ _____

6. Does your vision make clear how peers will be treated, both inside and outside of your unit? _____ _____

7. Do the people in your unit have a shared understanding of how support will be expressed in the unit, such as giving credit, celebrating successes, and so on? _____ _____

8. Does everyone in the unit understand and support how conflict and disagreement will be managed? _____ _____

9. Does your unit's vision clarify the desired balance between teamwork and individual contribution in the unit? _____ _____

10. Does everyone in your unit work from a clear set of values about how you will treat your customers? _____ _____

11. Does your vision make clear how your unit will keep on top of changing needs in your marketplace?  \_\_\_\_ \_\_\_\_

12. Does your vision stress the importance of learning and improvement when your unit fails to meet customer expectations?  \_\_\_\_ \_\_\_\_

13. Does your vision clarify how the people in your unit can help your customers operate more effectively?  \_\_\_\_ \_\_\_\_

14. Is your unit's vision idealistic?  \_\_\_\_ \_\_\_\_

15. Is your unit's vision achievable?  \_\_\_\_ \_\_\_\_

statement may or may not cover all of the points included in the checklist and not all of the questions will apply, but a good vision statement should address most of them. If you do not yet have a working vision, the checklist questions will provide you with useful information about what you need to think about in creating such a vision for your unit.

## Developing Your Visioning Competency

One of the main themes of this book is the importance of balancing competing managerial roles to accommodate diverse job demands. The strategic thinking and Visioning competency of the Innovator must be balanced with the detail orientation of the Integrator. Most of us have a natural preference for either details or the big picture, and given the way we are educated and rewarded as managers, the focus tends to be more on the former.

Given the traditional corporate preference for facts, details, and analysis, it is not surprising that creativity suffers.

It is not common practice to envision new and different products and services; the tendency instead is to perpetuate the status quo. Managerial mentors must be good at both envisioning the big picture and attending to details—seeing the forest through the trees and the trees through the forest.

Visioning as a learning leader requires creative thinking. There is a popular misperception that creativity is a quality that only artists possess and that such individuals are rare and distinct from the rest of the population. In reality, everyone has the potential to be creative, but most of us have not been encouraged to develop our creative ability. Creative thinking is about generating new ideas and solutions. It means questioning old assumptions and looking at things in a different way.

A vision is not a strategic plan; it is a tangible picture of the future. It is often said that the best way to predict the future is to invent it. Once you have envisioned your future, you can then move back into the present to determine what you need to do to realize that future. The process in Exercise 9 is often used by managers to develop their own and their co-workers' Visioning competency. Combined with the Visioning Competency Checklist in Exercise 8, going through this process will provide you with the tools you need to create an exciting vision of your unit's future.

To prepare to develop your vision, answer the questions in Exercise 9 about your organization as a whole. These questions are adapted from *Learning to Lead* by Bennis and Goldsmith (1994).

Bennis and Goldsmith suggest that by answering the broad-based questions in Exercise 9, you will be better prepared to create your vision. Choose a quiet and comfortable place and give yourself an uninterrupted block of reflection

## EXERCISE 9: **DEVELOPING YOUR VISIONING COMPETENCY**

1. Based on your experience as a manager in your organization, what have you learned? What has worked and what has failed? When have people been excited and motivated and when have they been turned off and discouraged? What is unique or special about your organization?

2. What are your personal work values; that is, what is most important to you about your work and your relationships with others, and how do those values affect your priorities for your future in the organization?

3. What could your organization do that would add value to the products and services that it currently provides its customers?

4. What would you most like to see your organization accomplish over the next few years in order for you to feel really good about yourself and your part in it?

time. Forget your practical managerial mind-set and try to create a dream of the future. Answering the questions in Exercise 10 will help you with that process. You may wish to write down your vision, speak into a tape recorder, describe it to someone else, or draw a picture of it. Or, you may choose just to dream about it.

The point of Exercise 10 is not to come up with a perfect picture or a precisely written document. The process is more important than the product. According to Robert Fritz (1991), what your vision does is more important than what it says.

As you think about the vision you have created, put yourself into the picture. As a learning leader, what do you want to be doing and what roles do you see yourself playing in the future? Becoming a managerial mentor means claiming your dream and making it a reality. Developing your Visioning competency is an excellent way to get started.

## The Championing Competency

Even in organizations where Visioning is practiced, there would be no innovation without someone to shepherd new ideas—or push others to shepherd new ideas—through the system. Championing, the second Innovator competency, involves using the learning leader's skills, strategies, and personal power to bring creative ideas into use. In her study of people she calls *change masters*, Rosabeth Moss Kanter (1983) describes how successful corporate entrepreneurs, by engaging in coalition building, develop a network of backers who agree to provide resources and support. Kanter's coalition builders act as cheerleaders with their peers while simultaneously pursuing the blessings of the top.

## EXERCISE 10: **CREATING A WORKING VISION**

1.  Imagine yourself in a helicopter hovering over your organization five years from now. How has the world changed and how does your organization fit into that changed environment? What kinds of products or services is your organization providing and how is it perceived by the outside world? What does it look like physically? How do people inside the organization feel about working there?

2.  As your vision begins to evolve, expand on it and flesh out the details until you have created a clear picture of the future. Do not try to edit or change it while you are creating it, just go with the flow and let it emerge.

3.  Now go back and go over the first two questions to make sure that you have included everything in your vision. You may wish to lay it aside and go back to it again later to see if there is anything else that you want to add to it.

4.  Once you feel that you have a good working vision, share it with your colleagues and get their reactions. As a learning leader, get them involved in your vision. Encourage them to create their own visions and share them with you and others.

5.  As other people create and share their visions with you and others, look for similarities and differences and try to come up with a shared vision of the future. If you are working as a team, you may wish to go through the questions together and try to create a team vision.

The managerial mentor's knowledge of how the system works is a distinct advantage in Championing. She knows how to build coalitions of those who need to "buy in" if the new idea is going to fly. Coalition building is not the same thing as moving systematically up the chain of command to get buy-in. Instead, it requires convincing managers of related functions, customers, and other stakeholders of an idea's value so they will not see it as a threat. This process often results in a kind of horse trading whereby the Innovator makes promises and offers resources in exchange for their support of the new project. To get top-level support, the Innovator must convince the powers-that-be of the technical and political viability of the new project, especially when the stakes are high.

Championing is more about managing organizational relationships than it is about technical know-how. If an Innovator has built the relationships necessary to get top management support, it is much easier to enlist the support of staff and peers in the project. Sometimes, however, the process works the other way around, and top management makes sign-off contingent upon the creator first obtaining peer resources and approval. In either case, the Championing competency involves knowing how to work the system and use one's personal power and influence to sell an innovation and negotiate for the resources needed to implement the project.

According to Peter Block (1987), coalition and support building call for two things: agreement and trust. People become adversaries or allies based on these two dimensions. Block claims that we either agree or disagree about where we are headed, and we either trust or distrust one another based on the way we operate in pursuit of that future. Block maintains that Championing first involves identifying all the people we need for the success of the project—bosses, peers, direct reports, customers—and assessing each individual on their perceived level of agreement and level of trust. This process results in the following five categories of people: Allies—high agreement, high trust; Opponents—high trust, low agreement; Bedfellows—high agreement, low trust; Fence Sitters—low trust, unknown agreement; and Adversaries—low agreement, low trust. Block suggests using this classification as a basis for dialogue with each individual. He makes the valuable point that until we actually talk with people, we cannot really know where they stand.

Block further suggests specific steps for negotiating relationships with each of the five categories of people with the goal of moving people into a high-trust, high-agreement mode. He thinks that most of our Championing efforts should be spent with current Allies or in the search for new ones. Engaging in the kind of joint Visioning process described in the last section is an excellent way to get Allies on board. The second focus should be on Opponents. By providing us with a sense of the marketplace for our ideas, they help us improve our act. Block says that the third priority should be Bedfellows, whose support we want but who require time and effort to build a higher level of trust. Fence Sitters are not worth our time and energy because they shift with the prevailing winds. Finally, if our initial attempt to dialogue with Adversaries is unsuccessful, Block says that if there is no progress after a second meeting, abort the effort.

## Championing in Practice

Thirty-two-year-old Laura Henderson has been employed as a marketing manager for a small, established high-technology company for the last nine years. The company, located in

North Carolina, has a reputation for not being state-of-the-art in the industry, preferring to go with its established product line. As a result, industry analysts have tended to view its future with skepticism, and a number of its key employees have left to join more innovative organizations. Laura, hired originally as a programmer, has worked her way up the corporate ladder in spite of being perceived as a maverick in a traditional male-dominated culture. Ever since joining the company, she has made it a practice to think about the future and experiment with ways to take advantage of emerging business opportunities. Her ideas, often considered revolutionary, have included dialogue groups with customers, internal information-sharing teams, and a corporate Web site. While commonplace today, her message early on was that to thrive in an increasingly fast-moving and competitive environment, the company needed to connect people and become more externally focused.

In spite of the raised eyebrows on the part of senior management, Laura has built a strong following among middle-level managers and technical staff. She has worked with the internal information-sharing groups to develop an innovative vision of the organization's future as well as several new product ideas that have generated a lot of enthusiasm among both her technical and managerial peers. The group has shared their efforts with a few key senior people, but the response has been indifferent at best.

With her outside contacts, Laura moved into the Championing phase by signing up her organization as a participant in a large industry gathering. By quietly promoting the meeting among key people in the company, a large number of people turned out, including a few senior management people. When senior managers saw the enthusiastic response on the part of their own people and especially their customers, they agreed to convene a task force to move forward with some of the group's new ideas.

Over the next year, the company tested the waters with a few of the new products. They were well received and went a long way toward improving the company's image in the marketplace. As a result, Laura was assigned to head up a new product development unit composed of many of her earlier allies in the original grassroots effort to revitalize the business. She is still perceived by many traditionalists in the company as a bit of a loose cannon, but they have to admit that she knows her business and gets results.

## Assessing Your Championing Competency

In the preceding example, Laura Henderson provides a good illustration of Championing in practice. Laura was a risk taker and thrived on new challenges. As you complete Exercise 11 on page 94, think about your own comfort level with risk taking and how such behavior is viewed in your organization.

Go back and look at which questions you responded to in the Yes column. Questions 3 and 6 deal with your organizational culture; if you responded in the affirmative to either of them, you need to do some serious thinking about how you can build needed support in a culture that may not value innovation. The rest of the questions relate to some of the personal characteristics associated with successful Championing. If most of your responses were in the affirmative, you need to concentrate on how to expand your Championing style flexibility.

## EXERCISE 11: **CHAMPIONING COMPETENCY CHECKLIST**

|  | Yes | No |
|---|---|---|
| 1. I prefer to stick to the tried-and-true and not make waves. | _____ | _____ |
| 2. People who are always questioning things are troublesome. | _____ | _____ |
| 3. Our organization places a high value on conformity. | _____ | _____ |
| 4. I analyze new alternatives very carefully before taking action. | _____ | _____ |
| 5. I believe that there is usually one right decision. | _____ | _____ |
| 6. Creative types are not particularly appreciated in our organization. | _____ | _____ |
| 7. I prefer security to novelty. | _____ | _____ |
| 8. I am not interested in revisiting a decision once it has been made. | _____ | _____ |
| 9. I like to act on facts more than hunches. | _____ | _____ |
| 10. I prefer to focus more on tasks than relationships. | _____ | _____ |

## Developing Your Championing Competency

Managing relationships is the key to developing Championing competency. The questions in Exercise 12, on pages 95—96, will help you build support and create new alliances.

## EXERCISE 12: **DEVELOPING YOUR CHAMPIONING COMPETENCY**

1. How often am I in contact with my peers? How could I benefit more from these interactions?

2. How often am I in contact with people in different parts of the organization? How could I benefit more from these interactions?

3. Among my direct reports, who appear to be the most promising? What more could I do to help them learn and develop on the job?

4. Who is the most influential senior person to show an interest in my work? How could I make my abilities even more evident to this person?

5. What could I do to be of assistance to this influential senior person?

## EXERCISE 12: **DEVELOPING YOUR CHAMPIONING COMPETENCY** (cont'd)

6. What contacts, both inside and outside of the organization, have the greatest potential value to me and the organization?

7. How can I use these contacts to support my objectives, exchange resources, or otherwise enhance my situation?

8. What new contacts could I make that would make me even more of an asset to the organization?

## The Diffusing Competency

Many attempts at organizational change are of a superficial nature. Major initiatives such as TQM and reengineering often result in limited change because their organizational sponsors do not know how to implement change. Learning leaders can develop Visioning and Championing competencies, but without Diffusing competency, transformation will not occur. Much of the problem is that managers take a mechanistic view of change and assume that there is a correct and orderly way to implement it. Because some organizational change models are more theoretical than operational and do not spell out the *hows*, managers underestimate the challenge and soon become disillusioned.

In fact, organizational change is a complex and messy process. Implementing new initiatives that require people to change traditional ways of thinking and acting demands a high level of Diffusing competency. In the Innovator role, Diffusing means spreading or disseminating a new initiative so that it becomes the accepted way of doing business. Diffusing, in many ways the most difficult of the Innovator competencies, is essential to implementing broad-based organizational change.

## Diffusing in Practice

Carl Washburn is the administrative vice president for a Connecticut-based chain of office supply retailers with locations in five New England states. The company, OfficeOne, has been on a fast growth track for the past five years in a highly competitive, change-driven business. During that time, Carl has worked extensively with the top management group to continually update the organization's vision and strategy in order to exploit new business opportunities. While Carl has always made a real effort to communicate top management's thinking to the rest of the organization, there has been concern expressed, especially by store managers outside of Connecticut, that they cannot understand or keep up with the constant changes. As a result, they tend to view any new initiative with suspicion and do not support needed behavior changes.

Carl decided to take a personal risk and make the visioning process itself a behavior change initiative. Instead of the top management group, he established multiple teams throughout the organization and assigned each of them a vision subtopic. The teams themselves agreed to enlist the ideas of other people throughout the various OfficeOne locations, and people were encouraged to experiment with new ideas immediately. The teams had a twin mandate; to develop a vision *and* get as many people as possible participating in the visioning process. Through Carl's initiative, their vision became a tangible reality for people, something that they could relate to and live *now*.

As they focused on a particular vision component—for example, personalized customer service—they learned and incorporated their learning into that vision component. Most important, necessary behavior changes occurred as a natural part of the process. Through his competence in Diffusing, Carl was gradually able to orchestrate a major organizational change and implement a motivating vision for OfficeOne.

## Assessing Your Diffusing Competency

Orchestrating a major organizational change takes a lot of courage. You must have both the self-confidence and the credibility to get others to believe in and support your change initiative. The checklist in Exercise 13 will help you think about your current level of Diffusing competency.

The more answers you have in the Yes column, the better. Remember, however, that many of these characteristics are best acquired through on-the-job learning. Even if you do not possess many of them now, you can begin to develop your Diffusing competency by trying out new behaviors in low-risk situations and learning from those experiences.

## EXERCISE 13: **DIFFUSING COMPETENCY CHECKLIST**

|  | Yes | No |
|---|---|---|
| 1. Do you have the self-confidence to carry through with your innovation when your role is unclear and the outcome is uncertain? | ___ | ___ |
| 2. Are you willing to share the limelight and let others take credit for your innovation? | ___ | ___ |
| 3. Will you speak out on a controversial issue surrounding your innovation when it may be personally risky to do so? | ___ | ___ |
| 4. Do you make it a point to become fully knowledgeable about all the factors that can potentially impact on your innovation? | ___ | ___ |
| 5. In promoting an innovation that calls for learning and practicing new behavior, do you walk the talk? | ___ | ___ |
| 6. Are you able to bounce back easily from failure and see it as a learning experience? | ___ | ___ |
| 7. Are you able to share your uncertainty and solicit advice from others when you are not sure what to do next? | ___ | ___ |
| 8. Can you take bold but risky action when needed to overcome a significant barrier to implementation of your innovation? | ___ | ___ |
| 9. Do you have enough credibility with key influencers for them to believe in the potential viability of your innovation? | ___ | ___ |
| 10. Do you have the patience and persistence to keep pushing your innovation in the face of repeated frustration and setbacks? | ___ | ___ |

## EXERCISE 14: **DEVELOPING YOUR DIFFUSING COMPETENCY**

1. What work experiences have required you to take a personal risk, and what was the outcome?

2. Who in your organization do you consider to be good at Diffusing, and what behavior have they demonstrated on the job that leads you to that conclusion?

3. Given your assessment of your current Diffusing competency, what steps could you take on the job to improve in this area, for example, getting involved in implementing a new project?

4. What outside activities could you get involved in that might help develop your Diffusing competency, for example, leading a change effort for a nonprofit organization?

5. How can developing your Diffusing competency enhance your job performance?

Developing Your Diffusing Competency

Exercise 14 provides you with an opportunity to reflect on your Diffusing competency and what you can do to enhance your skills in this area. Think about your current job and identify a few specific activities that might help you get some practice in taking risks and implementing change.

## The Innovator in Action

Howard Schultz, CEO of Starbucks, the number-one coffee retailer in the United States, is a true Innovator. Schultz grew up in a rough Brooklyn housing project, and after going through college on student loans and working as a Xerox salesman, he joined Starbucks in 1982. At that time Starbucks was a small Seattle coffee retailer, but Schultz envisioned a national chain of romantic espresso coffeehouses in the Italian tradition where *baristas* would custom-make each drink. Since Schultz bought Starbucks in 1987 and implemented his vision, the company has grown to nearly 1,400 coffee shops in a variety of locations, including shopping centers, airport terminals, and supermarkets. It also sells various food items and beverages and offers mail order and on-line catalogs. In 1997, its sales were $966.9 million, a 38.8 percent growth over a one-year period, and it employed 25,000 people.

The remarkable Starbucks story is told in *Pour Your Heart into It* (Schultz and Yang, 1997), a fascinating chronicle of an entrepreneurial CEO who combined coffee, commerce, and community into an innovative business. Starbucks has been built around the vision, values, and creativity of Howard Schultz. He has a real passion for everything about coffee and writes of "the romance of the coffee experience" at Starbucks. His core vision is that Americans are starving for someplace other than work or home where they can relax, engage in conversation, and build relationships, and that this desire for community can be met by local coffeehouses around the country.

In Championing his vision, Schultz did not have an easy time attracting financial backers. When he would try to explain to investment bankers that he wanted to build something more ambitious than a profitable enterprise, they typically tuned out. Their eyes glazed over as he described his vision of educating consumers about fine coffee and creating an atmosphere in his stores that drew people in and gave them a sense of romance in the midst of their overdriven lives. Schultz eventually acquired backers who shared his passion for his product and who envisioned the kind of organization he did, and the rest is history.

In building Starbucks, Schultz realized that his first priority had to be his people, since they would be the ones responsible for communicating the passion for coffee to their customers. He knew that if they did that well, they would accomplish their second priority of taking care of their customers. By achieving both those goals, they would create long-term value for Starbucks' shareholders. Schultz's diffusion strategy was to create what he called "bean stock," a stock option plan that turned every Starbucks employee into an owner. According to Schultz, even though people could not be sure that their options would ever be worth anything, they began to come up with innovative ideas about how to cut costs, increase sales, and create value. By linking shareholder values with long-term rewards for people, Schultz made clear the connection between their contributions and the growing value of the company. By placing as much importance on Starbucks' people as on its profits, and as much on creativity as on growth, Schultz not only talked about values and innovation, he walked the talk.

## Becoming an Effective Innovator

Although Howard Schultz eventually bought Starbucks and became CEO, he did not start the company; other people did. He took a small local business with six stores in Seattle and through innovative visioning, championing a dream, and diffusing ownership, transformed Starbucks into a phenomenally successful national enterprise in just a few years. As an Innovator, his story is informative for learning leaders at all levels.

The questions in Exercise 15 on page 104 ask you to think about what made Howard Schultz such an effective Innovator. You can then revisit your own Innovator competencies and create specific learning activities to help you become a more effective Innovator.

Innovation is essential to organizational transformation. It is a creative act that goes beyond adaptation; it takes existing circumstances and recaptures them in a new form. The primary purpose of innovation and change is to get results. Innovation is about performance, not change for its own sake. Clear performance targets bring skill changes to life for people who must learn new ways of thinking and doing. Whether the change is called innovation, reengineering, or TQM, people need to understand the relationship among purpose, performance, and change. That is the role of the learning leader as Producer, the subject of the next chapter.

## EXERCISE 15: **DEVELOPING YOUR INNOVATOR ROLE**

1. What about Howard Schultz's vision made it more than just a vague statement of a desired future?

2. How much do you think Schultz's espoused "passion" for his product contributed to his ability to effectively champion it?

3. How did Schultz demonstrate the Diffusing competency?

4. What was your relative preference for the Innovator role on the Learning Leader Preference Inventory, and which of the three competencies, Visioning, Championing, or Diffusing, do you need to focus on to improve your effectiveness as an Innovator?

5. What specific learning activities, on or off the job, might you undertake to become a more competent Innovator, and how might that enhance your overall job performance?

CHAPTER SIX

# The Learning Leader
# as Producer

UNFORTUNATELY, HIGHLY TOUTED performance improvement programs often have little impact on the bottom line. Managers wax enthusiastic about such programs as Continuous Improvement and Middle Management Empowerment, yet cannot demonstrate how such programs directly result in operational and financial improvement. One reason is that such programs are often activity based rather than results driven. The notion seems to be that if people aggressively engage in competitive benchmarking or breakthrough thinking, performance improvement will necessarily follow. The sad irony is that as organizations continue to spend millions of dollars on programs that fail to improve competitiveness, the very people that top management wants to empower become progressively cynical about the whole process. What these organizations fail to realize is that the only performance improvement initiatives that work over time are those that focus on the achievement of specific, measurable goals.

Another unfortunate reality is that in times of major change, organizational leaders often try to motivate people with lofty purpose statements and captivating visions. While well intended, such efforts draw attention away from a much-needed focus on performance. Inspirational messages are not without merit, but broad statements of purpose need to be translated into performance goals specifically targeted at the desired change.

Organizations that want to gain and sustain a competitive advantage must find ways to learn faster than the competition. While short-term performance is important—such as shipping high-quality products on time—the key to long-term success is continual learning. Learning leaders can enhance performance through breakthrough solutions or incremental improvement; either way, it is the continual search for a better way that adds value for the customer.

During difficult organizational transitions, learning leaders often feel pulled in opposite directions. They complain that they are caught between conflicting roles and that their organizations expect them to be empathic and supportive while always performance driven and improvement oriented. The reality is that in today's organizations, managerial mentors must be all of those things. In some situations, learning leaders must be directive; in others, they need to be collaborative; in a few situations, they must be both at the same time! The key to effectiveness in today's organizational environment is the ability to integrate and perform all four managerial mentoring roles of Collaborator, Innovator, Producer, and Integrator.

In *Why Change Doesn't Work*, Robbins and Finley (1996) describe four managerial approaches they call Pummel, Push, Pull, and Pamper. In their view, Pummel, described as martial law that might work in wartime emergencies, and Pamper, an extreme version of the New Age manager-as-good-guy, are short-term fixes at best. The former, they contend, leads to bureaucracy and the latter to chaos. Robbins and Finley think that successful organizational change lies in a combination of Push and Pull, and knowing when to use which.

Over the last few years it has become fashionable to label middle managers as change resisters. Called pencil-pushing, non-value-adding coordinators, middle managers have been prime targets for downsizing. Now, as organizations have become flatter and more process driven, middle managers are once again seen as potentially valuable resources with an important role to play in helping their organizations turn vision and strategy into bottom-line performance.

Sometimes called the revenge of the downsized, companies are once again realizing how important it is to cultivate and retain experienced management talent. Research carried out by Educational Testing Service showed that in the period from 1989 to 1995, contrary to popular belief, more jobs were created for business managers and professionals than for high-technology workers. The difference is that today's managers must focus equally on performance *and* people. In the Producer role, managers must be task-focused learning leaders committed to bringing out high performance in others. This demand for high performance is not a new theme; most experienced managers are reasonably familiar with the Producer role. Traditionally, however, the Producer role has often been used to justify coercion, intimidation, and threat. People have been forced to produce so many acceptable quality products in so many hours, so many of which are then sold to so many people resulting in so much of a contribution to an organization's bottom line. This is the Pummel style of management referred to earlier.

Pummel and Push techniques may work in the short term, but successful performance is more than a numbers game; it calls for delivering results of value to customers, shareholders, and employees. While short-term results may please shareholders, they do not necessarily make for satisfied customers or employees. Today, organizations must move beyond a short-term mentality and adopt a longer-term perspective that includes the impact of performance results on all three key stakeholders.

In the Producing role, managerial mentors serve as linchpins who connect marketplace realities, top-management strategy, and workforce initiative. As learning leaders, they set performance targets designed to maximize results. To do that, they must keep abreast of changing marketplace needs and continually learn, adapt, and align.

In a recent article on Silicon Valley in the *New York Times*, Esther Dyson (1998), head of Edventure Holdings, a venture capital firm, decries the fact that today everybody wants to be a CEO but nobody wants to do the grunt work of management, operations, and marketing. This problem is not limited to Silicon Valley start-ups. Many free agent managers in large organizations profess to be intrapreneurs, but have neither the skills nor the interest to see their ideas through to customers, develop collaborative teams, improve work processes, or strive for peak performance.

Fully competent Producers with responsibility for business units must make informed choices about what performance targets to set. To do that, they must understand their organization's broader vision and purpose and translate that knowledge into specific performance goals. Targeting, therefore, is the first Producer competency.

## The Targeting Competency

Even if people get excited or temporarily motivated by top management change rhetoric, it is wasted rhetoric unless managers understand what they need to do to help their organizations realize that change. Learning leaders must set performance targets for themselves and others and articulate the skill, behavior, and relationship changes needed to achieve important results. Lofty language alone will not motivate change; people need to learn how to perform in new ways or "business as usual" will prevail and no new learning will happen.

### Targeting in Practice

Joan Williamson manages a group of fifty human resource training consultants who work for a large management consulting firm based in Denver. The average age of the consultants is twenty-eight, and many of them have advanced degrees in management and organizational behavior. Because the firm has experienced rapid growth, particularly in team building consultation, the majority of the consultants are relatively new hires and have been with the firm for less than two years. Their work keeps them on the road most of the time, so they rarely get together as a group. As a result, Joan has not worked with them to establish many ground rules, and each consultant operates independently. Because their compensation is driven by the number of training hours they bill, most of their nondelivery time is devoted to getting new business.

For several months, Joan has been having an increasingly difficult time getting the consultants to bill clients promptly and follow up on receivables. Under the current compensation system, consultants are paid a base salary plus an incentive for the number of training programs delivered. They are responsible for getting billings to the consulting firm's accounting office as soon as a program has been delivered. The problem is that they are typically very slow with the paperwork, and as a result the firm has a chronic cash flow problem.

Joan has reminded the consultants on numerous occasions that it is their responsibility to bill promptly and follow up with clients to make sure that invoices are paid. The consultants have continued to drag their heels and complain that it damages their professional image to have to act as bill collectors. Joan has been getting a lot of heat from the senior partners, who are very concerned about the cash flow problem. They have made it clear that she needs to fix the problem immediately, or her job may be in jeopardy.

Put yourself in Joan's shoes and consider the following questions:

1. What is the underlying problem?

2. What specific actions could Joan initiate to resolve the problem?

3. Are new performance targets needed? If so, who should set them and what should be their focus?

4. What are some specific skill, behavior, or working relationship goals that Joan might set for herself or with the consultants to help resolve the problem?

Joan realized that the consultants perceived themselves as independent contractors who were paid to sell and deliver training programs. To build a sense of organizational identity, she convened a two-day off-site meeting with the consultants and, together with a senior partner, worked with the group to develop an understanding of the firm's business strategy and plans for the future. The consultants were shown how critical their efforts were to the success of the organization and how the cash flow problem was limiting the firm's ability to develop new products and grow in the highly competitive training and consulting marketplace.

Joan accepted that she needed to become a more effective hands-on manager and, to that end, initiated some personal development steps. She also created a volunteer task force of a few of the consultants to work with her to rethink their key accountabilities and clarify performance targets. She created other task forces to address such strategic marketing issues as how consultants might work with customers to identify emerging training needs and opportunities, and how to feed that information to the firm's program designers. To deal with the cash flow crisis, she put short-term incentives in place and the consultants responded almost immediately.

## Assessing Your Targeting Competency

The questions in Exercise 16 on page 112 will help you assess your Targeting competency. To be an effective Producer, you must be able to provide clear answers to each question. If you cannot do so, you need to work on your Targeting competency.

Notice that the questions cannot be answered in simple yes-or-no fashion. Go over your answers and think about your current level of Targeting competency.

## EXERCISE 16: **ASSESSING YOUR TARGETING COMPETENCY**

1. How do your work unit's performance targets specifically support the implementation of organizational strategy?

2. What kinds of performance initiatives have you put in place to target key improvement needs, such as cycle time reduction, customer value, and so on?

3. How have you determined that the people in your work unit understand and are committed to the unit's performance targets?

4. In what ways do your work unit's performance targets address your customers' unmet needs or unfulfilled expectations?

5. How do your work unit's performance targets address the need for continually updating people's knowledge, skills, and working relationships?

## Developing Your Targeting Competency

As a learning leader, one of your key tasks is to work with your unit to translate broad organizational strategies into specific unit performance targets. Top management may set the overall performance challenge, but you and your work team must determine your own performance targets and approach. The action steps that follow will help you think about ways you can enhance your Targeting competency.

### Work Unit Performance Targeting Action Steps

1. Develop your proficiency in the Collaborator role—in Facilitating, Coaching, and Dialoguing. You must be able to communicate openly and easily with the members of your unit if you want to build commitment to a common purpose.

2. Dialogue with the members of your unit to come up with a meaningful purpose for the unit that everyone understands and supports.

3. Drawing from broad organizational strategy and business objectives, set clear, simple, and measurable performance targets that everyone accepts as realistic and important.

4. Articulate a working approach that capitalizes on the skills and enhances the learning potential of everyone in your work unit.

5. Confirm that everyone is clear on individual and joint accountabilities and how progress will be monitored.

**113**

## The Improvising Competency

Learning leaders understand that organizational change demands continual improvisation. Work units can commit to ambitious performance targets but fail miserably if they do not learn by doing and make appropriate midcourse corrections. The Improvising competency relates to discovery learning, or learning by doing. Successful performance initiatives in times of change depend on people learning how to do things differently. That means experimenting with new approaches and finding out what does and does not work. In other words, in today's changing organizations, people can no longer afford to rely on what they already know.

An exciting new idea developed by the M.I.T. organizational learning group is the *practice field*. The M.I.T. research shows that managers need to engage in practice, much as people do in sports, the military, and the arts, if they want to become competent performers. While classroom training lacks direct relevance, practice fields provide people with opportunities to refine and test their skills under realistic conditions.

M.I.T. has put practice fields into place in a number of major corporations, including Ford and EDS. EDS set up a learning lab and helped a group of managers become proficient in the coaching skills needed in a learning organization. They provided a variety of different learning opportunities for participants to practice their new skills in projects where those skills could be applied to specific performance criteria. Peter Senge (1994), who was one of the creators of the concept of the learning organization, says that American managers have a tendency to grab onto the first feasible solution to a problem before adequately reflecting on the underlying causes. In the practice field environment, people have time to slow down and think and talk about what is really causing a problem. As a result, they are able to come up with better solutions based on firsthand skill practice and learning.

Improvising, whether in practice fields or through other learning techniques, helps people develop their performance skills and working relationships. Since learning means expanding people's capacity to do new things, it happens best when they actually *do* real things. You do not learn how to use a computer by reading a manual; you learn by using relevant material in the manual combined with live practice and reflection on how and why things work. While frustrating at times, the quality of learning by doing is far superior to classroom training in that people get a chance to see how their newly honed skills help them become more effective performers.

## Improvising in Action

A midsize Massachusetts bank wanted to provide its officers with a new learning experience. The CEO had seen the movie *City Slickers* and decided to send the group off to an Arizona cattle ranch to participate in a cattle drive and learn some basic cow-punching skills. His hope was that exposing his group of upper-middle-class Easterners to the unfamiliar challenges of life on the range would teach them how to improvise under difficult circumstances and learn how to operate as a team. Just as in Billy Crystal's film, the bankers got more than they bargained for and on more than one occasion found themselves at risk.

As they struggled with such tasks as stringing bales of barbed wire fence and keeping unruly cattle from stampeding, they came to the painful realization that nobody knew what to do because they had never done it before. When anyone tried to take charge, the result was usually disastrous, and that person became a source of great ridicule. When at one point they were faced with the imminently dangerous challenge of getting the cattle across a busy stream, someone finally suggested that they collaborate on improvising a process for getting man and beast across intact. Since nobody had any knowledge, skills, or experience to draw on, the group had to listen to each other and play out alternative scenarios in their minds.

With a little help from the trail boss, the bankers were able to come up with a successful solution, and both cattle and dudes survived. As a learning experience, this and other trail episodes proved invaluable; by having to improvise in unfamiliar and occasionally risky situations, the group had to learn how to operate as a team. As they reflected on the whole experience later, they realized that the challenges of banking in the twenty-first century might not be all that different from cattle driving. The old rules of banking were long gone, and teamwork and improvisation would be the keys to competitiveness—let alone survival.

## Assessing Your Improvising Competency

Think about a managerial situation in which you had to deal with a significant performance challenge that did not lend itself to a clear plan of action. You had to take immediate action even though you were not able to anticipate all the potential consequences ahead of time. It was an important but risky challenge that required you to experiment with different approaches in order to come up with the best solution. Now answer the questions in Exercise 17.

## EXERCISE 17: **ASSESSING YOUR IMPROVISING COMPETENCY**

1. What was the specific managerial situation and the significant performance challenge?

2. How did you feel at the time you had to take the risk?

3. How did you deal with the situation? Be specific.

4. What was the outcome and what were the major contributing factors?

5. How did you feel afterward about the way you dealt with the challenge, and what did you learn from it?

## Developing Your Improvising Competency

One of the important keys to developing your Improvising competency is to learn how to become a balanced risk taker. Balanced risk taking rules out unilateral action. One of the best ways to balance your risk factors is to dialogue with others, as demonstrated earlier in the example of the cow-punching bankers. Whether you tend to be an anxious or a careless risk taker, competent Improvising calls for learning how to strike a reasonable balance between the two. The following suggestions will help you think about how to develop your Improvising competence.

1. When you are facing a risky managerial performance challenge with significant unknowns, think through some if-then scenarios; but after a reasonable search, take action.

2. When you are thinking about a significant performance challenge, rely on your feelings as well as your reasoning.

3. Remember that there are no perfect decisions; you just want to find the best possible ones.

4. Seek out and consider new information, even if it may call for a new course of action.

5. If a performance challenge can have a potentially significant impact, take a reasonable amount of time to reflect on it ahead of time.

6. Try to anticipate potential positive and negative consequences while acting on the challenge.

7. Keep the dialogue going in real time by reflecting on what is and is not working, and why.

8. Encourage novelty and improvisation, but do not act rashly.

9. After completing a performance challenge, think about what was learned.

10. Reassure people that good attempts sometimes result in failure and that it is better to at least try.

## The Measuring Competency

The saying that what gets measured gets done is only partially true. In many ways, the measurement criteria used by organizations have not kept pace with changing times. Double-entry bookkeeping practices go back to the fifteenth century, yet such outdated methods are still favored by many management-by-the-numbers executives. Staff functions still rely on similarly outdated measures to maintain control and create reports that nobody reads. The performance review systems still used by many organizations provide a good case in point. It is still common to find systems that use a bell curve requiring that 5 percent of the workforce be rated as unsatisfactory, 20 percent as less than satisfactory, 40 percent as satisfactory, 20 percent as more than satisfactory, and 5 percent as highly satisfactory. It makes no sense today to predetermine that a certain percentage of the workforce has to be unsatisfactory performers, especially since many of these same organizations claim to hire and retain only the best people.

In recent years, it has become popular to measure customer satisfaction. For anyone who has answered such surveys, it often becomes readily apparent that the measure-ment criteria are not the ones that matter most to customers. Today, organizations are still inundated with measures that were more appropriate in another era. While initiating reengi-neering and other performance improvement initiatives, organi-zations continue to use outdated measurement criteria and pro-liferate useless reports. By developing their Measuring compe-tency, managerial mentors can rid their organizations of a lot of outdated measures and develop a few effective ones that matter.

Setting meaningful, measurable goals is one of the best ways to prevent organizational change initiatives from drift-ing into empty sloganeering. The first Producer competency, Targeting, is a precondition of meaningful goal setting. Trans-lating performance targets into simple, clear language that peo-ple can understand and relate to is no easy task, yet as organi-zations move toward more fluid, horizontal structures, rele-vant performance measures will become even more critical.

## Measuring in Practice

A respected New England clothing manufacturer dating back to the late nineteenth century was having serious problems. It had lost significant market share, and in spite of several orga-nizational improvement initiatives, the balance sheet was still in terrible shape and managers were demoralized. In keeping with the traditional culture, senior management did not share information about the seriousness of the situation until things became so critical that it was questionable whether the com-pany would survive.

Top management vacillated between ignoring unfavorable numbers and calling managers on the carpet. As a result, managers tended to hide problems and ignore the complaints of dissatisfied customers. With the help of an external consultant, top management realized that survival would require getting at the root causes of the problem.

Over the next year, effective performance measures were introduced that reflected the business strategy and objectives. These measures were directed toward specific goals and designed to provide managers with real-time problem-solving information. Through external benchmarking and other goals-related practices, managers became less insular and more focused on quality products and customer satisfaction. Top management, in turn, realized that creating meaningful, goals-based measurements and sharing information with managers paid off. As a result, their operational meetings became lively problem-solving encounters rather than passive cover-up sessions, and the company gradually regained its earlier position as a key player in the industry.

## Assessing Your Measuring Competency

As a learning leader, by choosing and using the right measures you will help people learn how to accomplish things they never thought they could do. You must select the right measurements, however; if you set unattainable targets, you will demotivate people, but if you set targets too low, people will not put forth the effort. Your goal should be to shift people from a What do I have to do? mind-set to a What can I do? mind-set. Exercise 18 on page 122 provides you with a checklist for assessing your Measuring competency. If you respond "no" to more than one or two questions, you need to take specific action to develop your Measuring competency.

## EXERCISE 18: **MEASURING COMPETENCY CHECKLIST**

| | Yes | No |
|---|---|---|
| 1. Do your measures have a demonstrable relationship to key performance targets? | ____ | ____ |
| 2. Do your measures reliably identify specific performance strengths and weaknesses? | ____ | ____ |
| 3. Do the names of your measures make it clear what is being measured? | ____ | ____ |
| 4. Can your measures be computed at a reasonable cost? | ____ | ____ |
| 5. Are all of your measures goals based? | ____ | ____ |
| 6. Do your measures have an external focus where possible? | ____ | ____ |
| 7. Are your measures directly tied to rewards where appropriate? | ____ | ____ |
| 8. Do you reevaluate your existing measures and update them from time to time? | ____ | ____ |
| 9. Do you use measures as a tool to implement change? | ____ | ____ |
| 10. Do the people in your work unit value and support your measures? | ____ | ____ |

## Developing Your Measuring Competency

Use the following ideas to think about ways to enhance your Measuring competency.

1. Inventory your performance measures to make sure that they are directly related to key performance targets, and discard the ones that no longer serve that purpose.

2. Develop measures that tell you how you are doing as well as how you did.

3. Use performance measures that measure learning and development as well as operations and finances.

4. Pilot the use of new performance measures before you implement the entire system.

5. Make sure that people are aware of your decision to no longer use a particular measure.

6. Change your reward and incentive systems to reflect measurement changes.

7. Link measures to what people do to contribute to targeted performance outcomes.

8. Make sure that performance data are easily accessible for measurement purposes.

## The Producer in Action

Ennis Lee is a team leader in an Indiana store that is part of a fast-growing drugstore chain with over seventy-five stores in several Midwestern states. The chain's organizational culture is based on decentralized teamwork, and each of the stores is an autonomous profit center with designated leaders and clear performance targets. The team leaders are expected to be true managerial mentors with Collaborating, Innovating, Producing, and Integrating competency. As Producers, team leaders are provided with complete financial information, and individual store performance figures are collected and shared throughout the organization.

Every day, Ennis posts a sheet showing the previous day's sales by team and another sheet with numbers from the previous year. Corporate also provides him with monthly information on profitability figures that anyone can request to see. He uses this information to track sales, and the teams provide input on pricing and ordering of products.

Ennis and his counterparts are given ambitious performance targets and are expected to meet or exceed their goals. Rather than exert top-down pressure to excel, top management fosters competition among peers so that teams not only compete against their own sales and productivity goals, they measure themselves against internal competitors.

Ennis and his associates practice a peer review system in which teams benchmark against each other. Team leaders visit different locations in other states and spend a lot of time socializing and sharing best practices. The organizational culture is a combination of democracy and discipline. As managerial mentors, Ennis and the other team leaders champion change and promote lateral learning—figuring out what other team leaders are doing right and carrying it back to the job. At the same time, they use hard numbers to provide ongoing performance feedback and foster healthy internal competition.

## Becoming an Effective Producer

Ennis and the other team leaders thrive in the Producer role. Think about your own Producer competencies in the context

## EXERCISE 19: **DEVELOPING YOUR PRODUCER ROLE**

1. What kinds of performance targets and measures currently drive the actions of the people in your work unit? Are they primarily results or activity driven? Individual or team based?

2. How can you act as a linchpin and focus your work unit's energy on performance targets that connect marketplace realities and top management aspirations?

of what you have learned in this chapter. As you consider the questions in Exercise 19 (pages 125—127), try to pinpoint your strengths as a Producer and what you can do to develop your managerial mentoring skills in this critical area.

As organizations move from command-and-control to team-based structures, team leaders must organize around people and process rather than around function. Their focus must shift from managing individuals to team performance and development. To do that, managerial mentors must become competent at organizational design. That is a prime challenge of the Integrator, the fourth learning leader role, and that is the subject of the next chapter.

## EXERCISE 19: **DEVELOPING YOUR PRODUCER ROLE** (cont'd)

3. How do your performance goals and those of the people in your work unit reflect the specific skill, behavior, and working relationship changes needed to meet new performance targets?

4. How can you build the practice of learning-by-doing into the work of your unit?

5. Where does your own job offer opportunities for targeting and measuring your performance more effectively? How do those opportunities relate to your scores on the Learning Leader Role Preference Inventory?

6. Which of the three competencies—Targeting, Improvising, and Measuring—do you need to focus on most to enhance your effectiveness as a Producer?

7. What specific learning activities, on or off the job, might you undertake to become a more competent Producer?

CHAPTER SEVEN

# The Learning Leader
# as Integrator

INTEGRATING SYSTEMS AND PEOPLE is not a new management task, but the role has become much more difficult in an era of increasing organizational complexity and change. With the need to rethink the ways they do business, managers have implemented many system changes, from the use of new technologies to business process reengineering. The results have often been disappointing. Since Hammer and Champy (1993) first introduced business process reengineering, management consultants have aggressively marketed numerous variations on the original concept. Hammer and Champy, however, concluded that 70 percent of reengineering efforts fail to achieve real results. While there are probably many reasons for failure, a major contributing factor has been inadequate attention to the human side of organizational change. Reengineering calls for changes in skills, behaviors, and working relationships, and as was pointed out in the last

chapter, organizations often make the mistake of implementing process design changes with insufficient attention to requisite new learning.

Effective managerial mentors avoid getting trapped in the
management fads of the day because they understand that
there is no simple approach to managing change. Learning
leaders know that a more complex managerial model is
needed, one that incorporates diverse and competing
demands. Change managers must be Collaborators, Innovators, Producers, and Integrators. They know that they must
perform all of these roles to integrate all the pieces; they must
create inspiring working visions, target performance results,
coach for understanding, and coordinate tasks that create
value for the customer.

Managers have traditionally resorted to reorganization
as the change strategy of choice. This is typical of the linear
management view that what worked in the past will work in
the future. Extrapolating the future from the past has contributed to the near downfall of many admired organizations,
as was demonstrated by the experience of some of the excellent companies first profiled by Peters and Waterman (1982)
in *In Search of Excellence.* In the years following the publica-
tion of that book, a number of the excellent companies cited,
including IBM, experienced significant problems, in part
because they kept doing the same things that had made them
successful in the past. Management critics often use the analogy of rearranging the deck chairs on the Titanic in describing
the frequent reorganizations undertaken by companies in the
name of strategic change.

Poor strategic vision was not the only source of IBM's
problems. While it is true that its predetermined course of
action caused it to fail to see the potential impact of the PC

revolution, it also failed to get managers in the divisions to think and act in new ways. IBM is an especially good example of what happens in the absence of strategic integration. Its managers, experienced professionals with excellent business savvy, remained stuck in the past.

The challenge for learning leaders as Integrators is to help people let go of the past, use old skills in new ways, and develop new skills. It does not mean abandoning the past; it means building on it.

Managerial mentors can be the key to effective strategy integration if they develop the competencies to translate strategy into action. They can serve as the link between various functional units and between top management and the rest of the organization. Their role is called Integrator because as learning leaders they must make sure that everyone in their work units understands the organizational strategy and its implications for them. As Integrators, managerial mentors must also carry information from their work units back to top management and serve as advocates for local strategies. As has always been true of linchpins, managerial mentors in the Integrator role often find themselves in the middle.

Robbins and Finley (1996) say that organizations are in the in-between age. They think that organizations will always be in the in-between age because they will continually need to sort out which aspects of the past to hang onto and which visions of the future are premature. According to them, the in-between age is not necessarily a bad place to be because it is where organizations can integrate a vision of the future with the wisdom of the past. If Robbins and Finley are right, the in-between age is an ideal setting for knowledgeable and experienced managerial mentors to practice the role of Integrator.

## The Organizing Competency

The old assumption was that the right organization design would result in the right performance. Traditional organization design involved defining job duties, determining spans of control, assigning people to boxes on organization charts, and grouping functions for coordination purposes. Today, organization design involves providing people with the tools and techniques they need to cope with unbridled organizational change. Rather than just structure, the emphasis is now on ways to improve performance through teams, training, and technology.

The Organizing competency still encompasses structural change, but of a different nature than traditional reorganization models. Fewer layers and flatter structures enable learning leaders as Collaborators to move from controlling to Facilitating, Coaching, and Dialoguing. Moving staff functions into the line, that is, returning human resource accountability to Producers, provides them with new opportunities for Targeting, Improvising, and Measuring performance. Creating small, focused work units provides Innovators with the Visioning, Championing, and Diffusing flexibility to respond rapidly to new business opportunities.

In practicing the Organizing competency, managerial mentors use new organizational designs to align people and performance. Instead of limiting themselves to the traditional practice of designing structure around strategy, they can now experiment with different forms and go with whatever improves performance. Organizing competency enables learning leaders to explore different organizing options for their own work units, even within large formal structures.

**132**

## Organizing in Practice

An example of the Organizing competency in action is the story of Jennifer Sorensen, the manager of systems support for a midsized semiconductor manufacturer located in a Southwestern city. With a workforce of over 1,500 people and growing, Jennifer and her group were under constant pressure trying to carry out their responsibilities for creating and maintaining the computer systems required to support the office, factory, and engineering needs of the plant.

Like many professional support groups, the systems unit felt caught between their two competing identities of skilled professionals and organizational members. Their jobs demanded a difficult skill mix of high-level technical expertise plus the ability to maintain good working relationships with their line clients. This difficulty was compounded by the fact that many of their clients were elitist technical professionals who tended to treat support personnel with thinly veiled contempt. The systems support group identified primarily with their professional role and spent a considerable amount of time attending computer conferences to keep abreast of changes in the field. They were attracted to such engagements because they found them considerably more stimulating than their internal client support activities.

Realizing that the cultural barrier between her staff and the line organization was having a significant impact on performance effectiveness, Jennifer determined that the need for professionalism had to be more in balance with the need for better integration between her staff and the line organization. To accomplish that, she organized a task force composed of members of both groups. The task force recom-

**133**

mended a number of integration strategies, including physically locating systems support staff close to line operations and, where interest and expertise permitted, rotating line people through staff jobs and vice versa.

Jennifer also enlisted the support of her internal organization development consultants to help her find ways to give line technical professionals a better understanding of how to exploit the resources and expertise of the systems support group. In addition, the organization development staff ran a series of consultative skills training programs for the systems support group and made themselves available for ongoing advice and support.

While Jennifer knew that there would probably always be a certain amount of tension between her staff and the line clients, she felt strongly that her decision to use an Organizing rather than a traditional conflict management intervention was the right move. Over time, the improved quality of systems support services and the more cooperative relationships between staff and line operations validated her decision. As a result, other staff service units in the organization adopted Jennifer's model, and in so doing, unnecessary and redundant processes were identified and eliminated. Equally important, members of the various staff support service units developed a new sense of ownership in the organization.

## Assessing Your Organizing Competency

The questions in Exercise 20 will give you insight into your current Organizing approach. For each item, select either alternative **a** or alternative **b.**

# EXERCISE 20: **ASSESSING YOUR ORGANIZING COMPETENCY**

1. Do you typically organize people around
   a. function
   b. process

2. Is the primary building block of performance
   a. individual work groups
   b. teams

3. Among the members of your work unit, are multiple competencies
   a. uncommon
   b. the norm

4. Is your basis for informing and training people typically
   a. need-to-know
   b. just-in-time

5. Do the people in your work unit have direct contact with customers:
   a. from time to time
   b. on an ongoing basis

6. Do you primarily reward
   a. individual performance
   b. team performance

7. Do you maintain cutting-edge professional and technical skills primarily through
   a. training
   b. ad hoc forums

8. Responsibility for overall process performance lies with
   a. management
   b. process owners

9. Do you worry more about span of
   a. control
   b. coordination

If you chose the **a** response for most of the items, your approach is more along traditional lines. That would not be surprising if you are working in a functional hierarchy. Even if that is the case, however, you can think of ways to pilot new Organizing approaches in your work unit.

## Developing Your Organizing Competency

Following are some suggestions for developing your Organizing competency.

1. Look at your organization through your customers' eyes. Do your customers understand how you are organized and how best to do business with you? Your internal organization should be transparent to your customers.

2. Focus on the core work of your unit. Get rid of narrow repetitive jobs and redesign them around what people need to do to meet or exceed customers' requirements. Design "whole" instead of fragmented jobs, enriched jobs that enable people to see how their work contributes to the big picture. Throw out old Taylorisms about division of labor between those who think and plan and those who act and do.

3. Find out from people in the unit what kinds of work tasks motivate them and try to build some of those factors into their jobs. Help them understand the end users' requirements and how their work contributes to customer satisfaction. Organize work so that support and control mechanisms are close to where the work is done in order for people to see the direct impact of their actions. Eliminate hand-offs policies wherever possible.

4. Evaluate existing policies, practices, and procedures for their current usefulness in supporting the core work of the unit, and get rid of those that do not meet that criterion. Let the people who actually do the work review their operations and suggest design changes that align them better with customer requirements.

## The Improving Competency

Managerial mentors must act as learning leaders for process improvement in their organizations. Traditional managers have derived their power more from the number of people reporting to them than from performance improvement efforts, and job evaluators have added job value points based on the former criterion. Reengineering has changed all that. With direct access to new information technology, people can now operate in decentralized, rapid-response teams that no longer require managerial oversight.

Improving is about eliminating the administrative underbrush that keeps people from doing their jobs and serving their customers. It is about developing systems and processes that support the achievement of important organizational goals and strategies. Too often, process improvement initiatives focus on learning statistical tools and techniques, with insufficient attention paid to helping learners figure out what they should be trying to improve.

The customer's experience of the product or service should be the starting point, with process improvements coming afterward. That calls for obtaining firsthand information from customers about their likes and dislikes and determining what kinds of improvements they feel would add significant value to the particular product or service. If customers do not

perceive the added value of a process improvement, it is questionable whether it is worth measuring. It is all too easy to
become enamored with measurement for measurement's sake
and to think that measuring in itself represents quality improvement.

Why have managers not taken a more active role in initiating systems and process improvements? While it is easy to
write them off as bureaucrats or change resisters, a more
likely explanation is that they do not know how to redefine
their roles to meet the changing needs of the new workplace.
Organizations as a whole have not done enough to help managers learn how to become learning leaders. In times of change,
they have provided transitional counseling and broad-based
organizational change workshops, but they have not provided
managers with the kinds of learning experiences they need to
become Collaborators, Innovators, Producers, and Integrators.
As a result, it is difficult for managers to act as change agents.
The following example is a good case in point.

## Improving in Practice

The case of Chris Johnson is an example of the difficulties
managers face in trying to carry out improvement initiatives.
Chris heads the administrative services arm of the Southwestern regional unit of a growing telemarketing organization
with headquarters in Philadelphia. Reporting to him at the
regional center are the human resource department, security,
purchasing, and payroll accounting. Chris, thirty-four years
old with a two-year college degree in communications, has
been with the company since it opened the Southwestern
regional office five years ago. In that period, he has moved up
from an entry-level job as client services representative to his

current position. Each of the units reporting to him is headed by an experienced manager, so Chris serves mainly as over-seer of operations and as a link to the regional director.

Recently, corporate headquarters in Philadelphia has put a lot of pressure on the regional offices to reduce administrative overhead and undertake process improvements to increase operating efficiency. They are particularly interested in exploring the possibility of using contract workers and out-sourcing payroll and security services. The regional director has instructed Chris to work with his unit heads and come up with a detailed process improvement plan within two months, with specific recommendations on the contracting and outsourcing issues.

Every time Chris has tried to initiate the planning process with the unit heads, they have let him know in no uncertain terms that they have more important things to do and that Chris is just letting the corporate staff people stick their noses into things they know nothing about. Because Chris is not intimately familiar with the actual work of the units, he can-not do anything without their involvement and support.

Chris is in the difficult position of many managers of administrative units comprising miscellaneous staff func-tions. Such functions are often a senior management target for process improvement, based on the common perception that they are staffed by unresponsive bureaucrats intent on con-trolling the efforts of those doing the real work of the organi-zation. Part of the problem is that managers of staff units tend to think in terms of functions rather than outcomes, and when called upon to justify their existence, they describe activities rather than outcomes. In order to move forward in the Integrator role, Chris will need to use his Collaborator, Innovator, and Producer competencies to refocus his unit managers on the administrative unit's mission, who their customers are, and how to satisfy their needs.

Improvements cannot happen unless and until the unit's mission becomes clear and tangible to the unit heads and they get actively committed to the process. The staff unit heads and Chris need to think of themselves as learning leaders who serve, not bureaucrats who administrate.

## Assessing Your Improving Competency

Answering the six questions in Exercise 21 will help you assess your Improving competency. Think about each question and try to come up with specific examples of how you currently demonstrate the Improving competency.

If several of your answers are in the No column, you need to work on ways to develop your Improving competency. Keep in mind that the people in your unit should be actively involved in determining the purpose of your unit, how the work gets done, who is accountable for what, where im-proved coordination is needed, and what new competencies are required to ensure quality.

## Developing Your Improving Competency

There are many ways to initiate process improvements. As a learning leader, here are some things that you can do. Improve your processes by finding ways to

- Eliminate mistakes, redundancies, and delays
- Do things faster and more easily
- Avoid waste of time and resources
- Rearrange or eliminate steps

## EXERCISE 21: **IMPROVING COMPETENCY CHECKLIST**

|  | Yes | No |
|---|---|---|
| 1. Does your unit mission statement make clear who your customer is? | ___ | ___ |
| 2. Does your unit mission statement describe your value to the customer and the ways you deliver that value? | ___ | ___ |
| 3. Do you evaluate and update your work processes to meet customers' changing needs and requirements? | ___ | ___ |
| 4. Are your work systems flexible enough to accommodate change? | ___ | ___ |
| 5. Do you determine the current efficiency of work systems before you computerize them? | ___ | ___ |
| 6. Do your process improvements have a clear focus? | ___ | ___ |

- Do things in parallel rather than sequentially
- Reduce cycle time
- Reduce the number of people the customer has to deal with
- Improve the information flow
- Eliminate useless information

Start with one or two important process improvement initiatives rather than attempting to do everything at once. That is the best way to build understanding and support for the effort. If you decide to use external consultants, remember that Improving is an important learning leader competency and that you should not make the common mistake of turning the effort over to consultants. The people in your unit who actually do the work are your best resources for process improvement.

## The Bridging Competency

Bridging is the third Integrator competency. Managerial mentors create effective working relationships by building bridges between groups. Often, organizational units view each other as competitors for scarce dollar and human resources. This is particularly true in traditional bureaucracies where turf battles are the norm and there is little apparent cooperation between groups. Yet anyone who has worked in a large bureaucracy knows that cooperation between people in different units happens informally, and that through these connections work gets done. People share ideas and solutions, but making informal connections is not typically in their job descriptions. These connections are the informal networks that are part of every organization.

With emerging technologies such as fax machines, e-mail, and so on, it has become much easier to share information and know-how across organizational boundaries. In today's global economy, that ability provides an important competitive edge. In the past, splitting organizations into specialized units produced impressive results, as in the case of the mass shipbuilding techniques used in World War II. But as Harvard Business School researchers Lawrence and Lorsch (1986 [1967]) have been pointing out for many years, segmenting an organization can also lead to serious communication and cooperation problems between different organizational units.

Traditional hierarchies, differentiated into various functions and departments, are integrated when units work well together and work is passed along in linear fashion from one unit to the next. The lines and boxes of the familiar organization chart reflect the differentiated organization, and until recently, this was the common organizing principle in corporate America. In the new economy, with the need for cross-functional communication and team collaboration to accomplish new tasks, the traditional organization chart will eventually become an anachronism. It will be replaced by the network organization, in which integration rather than differentiation is key, and multidisciplinary teams rather than functions and departments will be the basic organizational unit. The entertainment industry, in which teams of diverse talents are assembled to produce a film or a TV special and then disbanded to move on to other projects, is an example of organizational networks in practice.

Network organizations have the flexibility to continually adapt to changing environments and the ability to quickly accommodate new marketplace needs. In describing the Improving competency in the last section, we discussed the importance of using customer feedback as a foundation for the design of improvement projects. Managerial mentors typically acquire this type of information through Bridging.

Managerial mentors do not work in isolation. They function interdependently using the information available to them through their relationships with others. Today a strong network is considered an essential ingredient in managerial effectiveness. Harvard professor John Kotter (1982) describes a *network* as all the people both inside and outside of a manager's organization on whom he or she depends to get the job done. Learning leaders use networks for Bridging purposes.

## Bridging in Practice

The actions of Hank Sanderson, a forty-six-year-old director in a Midwestern health insurance company, provide a good example of Bridging. The company's senior management was getting many complaints from its field agents that prospective policyholders were frustrated and angry about the excessive amount of time between application and issuance of new policies. The agents blamed what they labeled the underwriting bureaucracy, the underwriters blamed the agents for submitting incomplete information, the policy issuance group blamed the underwriters for sending them large batches of approvals all at once, and so forth down the line.

Hank, a director in underwriting, volunteered to convene a task force of representatives from the involved units to work on the problem. Hank enjoyed an excellent reputation within the organization because of his repeated efforts to build relationships both inside and outside of underwriting and to provide support to others. He had made it a point to learn about how other parts of the organization worked and was fully convinced of the value of interdependent action.

Hank had the trust and respect of everyone in the group. He was able to help them see that it was in their own and the organization's best interests to get the new policies to their customers in a shorter period of time. To accomplish that, the members of the task force had to network within their own units and apply their best negotiating skills to get people to cooperate. Collaboration in the service of doing a better job to meet customer needs became the rallying cry, and after several months of formal and informal problem-solving sessions, the task force came up with a way to improve the information flow and significantly reduce policy issuance time.

The task force could not have achieved its purpose without Hank's Bridging competency. As valuable as the reduction in policy issuance time was, the fact that task force members were able to coalesce into an effectively working network was an equally important breakthrough.

## Assessing Your Bridging Competency

Exercise 22 on page 146 provides you with an opportunity to assess how well you currently practice the Bridging competency. Bridging is an increasingly important competency in today's workplace, so think carefully about your responses to each of the ten questions in this exercise.

If you have several No responses, you need to work on your Bridging competency. The next section will provide you with some suggestions for things that you can do.

## Developing Your Bridging Competency

As a managerial mentor, it is helpful to think of yourself at the center of a large web of people, both inside and outside of your organization, with whom you interact. In *The Web of Inclusion*, Sally Helgesen (1995) compares organizational webs to a spider's web that is both a structure and an evolving process. This interconnected web of relationships is essential to your ability to be an effective learning leader. Bridging is about building and maintaining those relationships in the web.

Your relationships in the web are not limited to other managers. Anyone in the organization can be a part of your network. Learning leaders do not build such relationships for selfish reasons; they believe in the value of helping others

## EXERCISE 22: **BRIDGING COMPETENCY CHECKLIST**

| | Yes | No |
|---|---|---|
| 1. Do you find it personally rewarding to collaborate with others? | ____ | ____ |
| 2. Are you good at remembering people's names? | ____ | ____ |
| 3. Do you have a genuine interest in other people? | ____ | ____ |
| 4. Are you able to put people at ease? | ____ | ____ |
| 5. Can you comfortably give without expecting something in return? | ____ | ____ |
| 6. Do you volunteer your time to charitable causes? | ____ | ____ |
| 7. Do you feel comfortable accepting help from others? | ____ | ____ |
| 8. Do you like to act as a referral source to others? | ____ | ____ |
| 9. Are you willing to share resources with others? | ____ | ____ |
| 10. Do you make it a point to remember information people give you? | ____ | ____ |

and feel that it makes good business sense. As Hank Sanderson's case demonstrated, Bridging through networking can pay dividends for everyone concerned.

Use the checklist in Exercise 23 to think about ways to develop your Bridging competency.

# EXERCISE 23: **BRIDGING COMPETENCY DEVELOPMENT CHECKLIST**

|  | | Yes | No |
|---|---|---|---|
| 1. | I actively engage in networking both inside and outside of the organization. | _____ | _____ |
| 2. | I participate in informal gatherings for networking purposes. | _____ | _____ |
| 3. | I have a reputation as someone to connect with in the organization. | _____ | _____ |
| 4. | I am actively involved in professional groups in my field. | _____ | _____ |
| 5. | I know who the people are in my network and how I can help them. | _____ | _____ |
| 6. | I make it a point to build and maintain my network on a regular basis. | _____ | _____ |
| 7. | I can demonstrate how networking improves my managerial effectiveness. | _____ | _____ |
| 8. | I make it a point to share information and expertise with others. | _____ | _____ |
| 9. | I feel comfortable calling on others in my network for help. | _____ | _____ |
| 10. | I actively network with my customers. | _____ | _____ |

If you answered Yes to most of the items, you are already actively Bridging. If not, go back and review your No responses to determine what else you can do to develop your Bridging competency.

## The Integrator in Action

A large state agency in northern New England was faced with the need to reorganize its headquarters and field staff to cope with funding cutbacks. Department heads were anxious to explore alternatives to staff reduction, especially in field offices, because of increasing client demand for the agency's services due to local funding cutbacks and poor economic conditions in the region.

As head of the agency for eight years, forty-one-year-old Janice Armstrong had already gone through several reorganizations, all of which caused serious morale problems and led to poorer-quality client service. This time, she was determined to try something different in the hope that staff would be better prepared to cope with the change. Rather than working solely with her department heads, as she had in the past, Janice decided to work with representatives from the affected groups to see if they could come up with a reorganization blueprint that would meet cutback needs without reducing the quality of service to clients. She made it a point to include lower-level staff who worked directly with clients, such as field representatives and administrative support staff.

An external consultant helped Janice design a process to get the advisory group organized and identify the various options. From that point on, however, Janice took over, and the consultant was brought in only on occasions when the group needed specific technical support on human resource or organization design issues. After several weeks of intensive work, the group came up with a reorganization blueprint that would not entail a major reduction in force or in service to clients if—and only if—both headquarters and field staff were willing to accept other possible options. The options included job enlargement, staff furloughs, and attrition. The group broke into small cross-functional teams to present their recommendations to the rest of the agency for reactions and additional input.

After receiving brief training in facilitation, the teams worked with the rest of the agency staff over the next couple of months and then reconvened to come up with a final set of recommendations. Their final recommendations included a few new options suggested by agency staff and would enable the agency to live with the funding cutbacks without having to eliminate jobs or disrupt service to clients.

Throughout the entire reorganization planning process, Janice offered ideas and support to the groups but made it clear that it was their project. She was visible and available at all times, and through her formal and informal networks kept lines of communication open and people apprised of progress. As a result, the reorganization was carried out with few problems and no surprises. For the first time, the agency was able to break down traditional bureaucratic walls and work together to resolve a threat to the entire group. Equally important, they were able to shift their sole emphasis from how to protect their individual fiefdoms to how to best continue serving their clients.

## Becoming an Effective Integrator

In this chapter, you learned about several managers who successfully practiced the Integrator competencies of Organizing,
Improving, and Bridging. Think about your own Integrator
competencies as you consider the questions in Exercise 24 on
pages 151—152. Keep in mind that the Integrator role is
going to become increasingly important as organizations try to
break down bureaucratic walls and create new internal and
external links that will enable them to realize their full potential. Networking will be one of your keys to success as a
twenty-first-century learning leader.

In the last four chapters, you learned about the managerial
mentoring roles of Collaborator, Innovator, Producer, and
Integrator. If you are like most experienced managers, you
probably have a stronger preference for some roles than others. To become a learning leader, you will need to become
fully competent in all four roles. That means you will need to
design new learning experiences and acquire the flexibility to
apply different combinations of mentoring skills in diverse
change situations. In a real sense, you will need to learn how
to mentor yourself before you can mentor others. In the next
chapter, you will see how to leverage your knowledge, experience, and managerial wisdom and develop a learning plan to
become a twenty-first-century learning leader.

THE LEARNING LEADER AS INTEGRATOR

# EXERCISE 24: **DEVELOPING YOUR INTEGRATOR ROLE**

1.  When you hire new people, do you look for networking skills such as ability to make contact and build relationships, or do you focus more on technical knowledge and skills?

2.  What are some specific jobs in your unit that require networking ability and what, if anything, do you need to do to help those individuals acquire the necessary skills?

3.  Do you see yourself as more of a specialist or generalist manager? If the former, what can you do to acquire the generalist skills that will enable you to become more of a bridge builder?

4.  Do you mostly rely on impersonal forms of communication such as e-mail and voice mail, or do you spend considerable time interacting with people to get information and deal with important business issues? What can you do to increase your face-to-face interactions with people with whom you need to have good relationships?

## EXERCISE 24: **DEVELOPING YOUR INTEGRATOR ROLE** (cont'd)

5. Does your office layout promote easy interactions among people? What can you do to create a more open layout?

6. Do the people in your unit have a clear understanding of your unit's vision and mission and how it relates to the larger organizational strategy? If not, what do you need to do to rectify the situation?

7. What kinds of process improvement initiatives might enhance your unit's performance? How do these opportunities relate to your scores on the Learning Leader Role Preference Inventory?

8. Which of the three competencies—Organizing, Improving, or Bridging—do you need to focus on to enhance your effectiveness in the Integrator role?

9. What specific learning activities, on or off the job, might you undertake to become a more competent Integrator?

PART THREE | **PUTTING YOUR PLAN TOGETHER**

CHAPTER EIGHT PROVIDES AN OVERVIEW of what the organization of the future will look like and why continual learning will be so essential to organizational success in the coming century. The importance to learning leaders of receiving ongoing performance feedback is discussed with an emphasis on the increasing use of the 360-degree process for obtaining performance feedback from supervisors, peers, direct reports, and customers. The organization life cycle is described to help managerial mentors determine the stage that best matches their organization. A comprehensive set of assessment tools is provided to help prospective learning leaders put together a role competency development plan and task alignment strategy for their individual work units.

Chapter Nine links the concept and practice of managerial mentoring to Robert Greenleaf's (1977) concept of servant-leadership and shows how the two share a common principle base of serving people and building communities of purpose. The servant-leadership model provides learning leaders with a values framework for their work as Collaborators,

Innovators, Producers, and Integrators. The importance to managerial mentors of developing a servant-leadership mindset is discussed, and numerous examples are provided of successful organizations that practice Greenleaf's philosophy. The emerging popularity of the productivity-oriented concept of open-book management is discussed to show how it can be successfully linked to servant-leadership. The book concludes with a recap of the challenges facing twenty-first-century managers and shows how the practice of the four managerial mentoring roles can help build new organizational learning communities.

CHAPTER EIGHT

# Learning to Become
# a Learning Leader

A MAJOR THEME OF THIS BOOK is that twenty-first-century organizations will need managerial learning leaders. With leading-edge organizations moving from hierarchical to horizontal structures, managers must loosen the controls and concern themselves with lateral relationships and how to handle diverse and competing managerial demands. Today, many organizations in transition are hybrid structures with process responsibilities superimposed on existing hierarchies. This is particularly true in organizations that have implemented reengineering projects while leaving traditional controls and reward structures in place.

With the emerging shift to process-driven structures, managers are expected to coach more than control. The problem is that with recent downsizing cutbacks, managers are often faced with wider spans of control and fewer resources. As a result, they are often overburdened and have little time to spend coaching people. Not only are they expected to coach, they are also expected to carry out other time-consuming managerial responsibilities, such as attending meetings, doing project work, improving customer service, meeting performance goals, and more. The problem is exacerbated by the fact that many managers have technical or operational backgrounds and are neither interested nor skilled in coaching. Add the fact that compensation systems often do not place high value on coaching skills, and it is not surprising that managers are reluctant coaches.

It is clear that moving from hierarchical to horizontal structures will require more effective teamwork and that people at all levels will need to practice new learning on the job. Formal training will not be abandoned, but it will be different. Classroom training will give way to on-line training that will be more job related. An innovative example of this new approach to training appeared in the *Harvard Business Review* (Kelley and Caplan, 1993). Bell Labs, in an attempt to define the difference between star performers and average workers among engineers, had star engineers develop an expert productivity model that identified and ranked nine work strategies, such as taking initiative, networking, and self-management. Average performers, when asked to rank the same strategies, came up with a different order than the star performers. Bell determined that the real difference between the two groups was not IQ, but the ways top performers did their jobs. A productivity training program was developed and run by engineers using hands-on materials such as case studies and work-related exercises. The program led to significant productivity increases in both the star and average performers, and the message came through loud and clear: To increase productivity in the knowledge economy, managers need to focus more on people than on technology. The Bell Labs engineers, as managerial mentors, passed their skills along to others and performed as true learning leaders. The Bell experience represents the training wave of the future.

## Feedback for Learning Leadership

Individually based performance feedback systems have not been particularly successful. The tradition of the annual performance review has been a bone of contention between managers and their associates. When work processes are poorly defined and people are inadequately trained—a not-uncommon occurrence—it becomes virtually impossible to provide useful feedback. If traditional, individually based performance feedback has been of limited usefulness, it is reasonable to assume that it will be even less useful in new, team-based settings.

The fact is, good feedback can lead to performance improvement. In his book *Managing for the Future*, Peter Drucker (1993) went back in history and pointed to sixteenth-century church leaders Loyola and Calvin, who cited feedback as the primary key to learning. It is ironic that in spite of emerging evidence to support that early view, organizations still do not use constructive feedback to help learners understand their strengths and improvement needs. Studies show that people want to know how they are doing and that feedback can be a very useful instructional tool. The key lies in designing feedback systems that enable people to take personal responsibility for their own learning.

As a learning leader, to give and get good feedback you need to be forthright about opening up communications with people. That means more frequent interaction with both individuals and teams. It can range from asking open-ended questions about how the work is going to your taking over the role of client representative for a day. Whatever the process, it will send an important message to people about how you view the importance of their work. Used for live, on-the-job coaching, feedback can be a very positive learning tool.

Effective managerial mentors make it a practice to share their own learning experiences, including their mistakes, with others. By so doing, people will be less apt to cover up their own mistakes and will see you as a model for taking personal responsibility for one's own actions. Another good tactic is to ask your team for feedback. It provides you with invaluable data about how you are seen by others. Because giving leaders candid feedback can be viewed as high risk by team members, here is a suggested approach:

1. Ask each individual on the team to come up with a few critical incidents illustrating your positive behaviors and those you might improve on. Meet with them one-on-one and ask them to explain the impact of those behaviors on them and on the team.

2. When you have met with everyone, summarize the feedback and report your findings back to the team. Allow discussion time for clarification purposes and then share your personal development plan with the team and ask for their support.

3. If you are not comfortable with that process or think it would be too threatening to the team, use an outside person to interview the team and provide you with a summary report.

The important thing to remember is that you are not only asking for useful feedback for yourself, you are modeling a process that will make it more comfortable for other people to seek that kind of information for their own personal development.

A new performance development system that is becoming increasingly popular is called 360-degree feedback. A few years ago, few people had heard of 360-degree feedback, let alone practiced it, but now it is being embraced by private, public, and social sector organizations. The 360-degree feedback process involves soliciting performance or developmental feedback from associates who have direct knowledge of a manager's work behaviors. It is viewed as more valid and reliable than single-source supervisory appraisals. Organizations report that 360-degree feedback from credible associates can be a powerful force for positive behavior change. Associates can include supervisors, peers, direct reports, and internal and external customers. Managers receiving multisource assessments of their knowledge, skills, and working relationships frequently gain a rich understanding of their strengths and development needs.

A major advantage of the multisource assessment process is that the person under assessment is accountable to multiple stakeholders rather than to just one supervisor. This type of feedback is not a substitute for other performance management tools; in fact it often is used in conjunction with other tools. While other performance management tools typically focus on performance results, 360-degree feedback puts the emphasis on how people do their jobs. It enables managers to receive direct feedback that they might not otherwise get for fear of reprisal, and this information can serve as a sound basis for the development of individual learning plans.

There are a number of formal and informal approaches to such feedback. One purpose of 360-degree feedback

systems is to provide people with high-quality information for personal learning and development. It is very important that such systems be carefully implemented. When
poorly introduced, they can compound the perception of sub-
jectivity that plagues traditional performance appraisal
systems.

It is not our purpose to suggest that as a learning leader
you should initiate an organizationwide 360-degree feedback
system. That is a major undertaking requiring top management commitment, careful project design, and extensive employee communication and training. An alternative that is
open to you as a managerial mentor, however, is the use of
one application of the 360-degree process to get developmental feedback on your learning leader competencies. Based on
extensive research carried out by the Center for Creative
Leadership (Van Velsor and Leslie, 1991), one assumption is
that people who work closely with you can facilitate
your personal development. In this type of application, your
immediate manager is not involved in the process and
does not see the developmental feedback. The feedback
thus remains developmental and is uncoupled from performance. Assessors can provide candid responses because
they know that the information is confidential and solely
for developmental purposes, and there is no incentive to provide destructive information. The 360-degree feedback
process is currently used for leadership development in
such major corporations as Motorola, Intel, American
Airlines, and GMAC. If properly implemented through
careful design, user training, and confidentiality safeguards, 360-degree feedback can serve as an excellent development tool.

## Learning and the Organizational Life Cycle

You cannot get to your desired destination if you do not first know where you are. Therefore, one important step to becoming a managerial mentor is to assess where your group or organization is in the life cycle. Organizational theorist Wayne Baker (1994) describes six stages of growth, with organizations facing predictable crises at each stage. As you read the following adaptations of Baker's six stages and their crises, try to pinpoint where your organization or business unit is in the life cycle. The six stages are:

**Stage One:** This is the start-up stage where organizations are highly creative and full of entrepreneurial energy. Many high-tech firms fit this pattern and are founded by charismatic leaders like Steve Jobs at Apple Computer. They tend to be loosely structured and more like informal social groups. Relationships are casual and there are few formal controls. The crisis occurs when fast growth creates the need for professional management skills, and it becomes time for the founder to step aside.

**Stage Two:** In this stage, the professional managers begin to standardize operations and often redesign the organization. New controls stifle spontaneity and flexibility, and managers begin to act like specialists. Things get politicized and people fail to cooperate. People become very turf conscious so there is little collaboration. Bureaucracy becomes the norm, and the crisis comes when managers try to free themselves from bureaucratic constraints. To deal with the crisis, managers must build cross-functional bridges and delegate.

**163**

**Stage Three:** Delegation means converting the organization from a centralized to a decentralized structure. The functional structure is replaced by profit centers that are better able to cope with size and complexity, and new bridges are built across functions. The crisis occurs when managers who have focused on strategic rather than operational issues realize that they are too removed from the action. There is little coordination across organizational units, and the organization is more like a conglomerate. The challenge is how to create more coordination without recentralizing.

**Stage Four:** Changes at this stage involve merging decentralized units into product groups, building up headquarters staff, creating formal planning and coordinating procedures, and so on. These actions contribute to new growth due to increased efficiency and resolution of conflict between groups. The crisis is brought on by overcontrol and struggles between staff and line. The heavy focus on coordination stifles informal networking and red tape proliferates.

**Stage Five:** This is the stage many organizations have found themselves in since the early eighties. In an attempt to reduce bloated structures through massive layoffs, some organizations went too far and cut out muscle along with fat. Downsizing helped others refocus their core competencies. Problems arose when experienced people who had long-standing relationships with customers were gone and overburdened survivors had to pick up the pieces. Valuable organizational memory was lost. Traditional top-down controls no longer worked, and managers did not know how to revitalize people.

**Stage Six:** At this stage, networking is viewed as the best way to rebuild organizations and eliminate the negative effects of downsizing. Networking practices include relationship building, multi-functional teams, and partnering. Teamwork is a particularly critical component in helping people learn how to contribute in new ways. The crisis occurs over the failure to recognize the need for cross-team integration. Reintegration is achieved by building a network of teams to reduce duplication of effort and lack of coordination with customers.

As you think about your own organization or business unit, what stage seems to best match your current situation? Are you in the middle of a crisis in one stage, or are you in transition between stages? It is important for you to figure out where you are now so that you can act in ways that are appropriate to the needs of your organization. If you are in the middle of a crisis or anticipate that one is imminent, you need to act soon. If you are in a calm period between crises, you have more time to analyze the situation and plan accordingly.

Many organizations today are trying to move out of Stage Five, the downsizing stage, into Stage Six, the networking stage. The need to revitalize people and improve performance represents a formidable challenge to managers. There is an abundance of evidence that organizations have achieved mixed results at best for the millions of dollars spent on revitalization efforts. A recent study by the Harvard Business School found that while virtually all the Fortune 100 companies implemented at least one change program between 1980 and 1995, only 30 percent of those initiatives produced a bottom-line improvement that exceeded the company's cost of capital, and only 50 percent led to an improvement in market share price. This occurred despite the fact that each of the companies spent one billion dollars on change programs over the fifteen-year period.

There is no question that managers have devoted count-less quantities of time and energy to programs designed to empower people and improve quality. In a recent article in the *Harvard Business Review*, psychoanalyst and management writer Abraham Zaleznik (1997) worried that today, under the guise of empowerment, managers may be using task forces to sidestep their "real work" of thinking about and acting on ideas relating to products, markets, and customers. That is why the managerial mentoring model has so much potential for positive change; it calls for *balancing* the diverse demands of the four competing managerial roles, each of which is criti-cal to effective organizational performance. In the same *Har-vard Business Review* issue, Pascale, Millemann, and Gioga (1997) wrote that a major reason for the limited success of many change management programs is that the whole burden of change rests on too few people. In their words: "The num-ber of people at every level who make committed, imaginative contributions to organizational success is simply too small. More employees need to take a greater interest and a more active role in the business. More of them need to care deeply about success" (p. 127).

These authors are saying that revitalization requires real change in on-the-job behavior. That is not an incremental process, and it requires a thorough resocialization of people so that they feel they are working for a new and exciting organization.

A major problem with many organizational transforma-tion models is that they are too abstract and difficult to trans-late into action. Pascale, Millemann, and Gioga tracked a number of change efforts and found that there were three practical interventions that worked: actively involving people in the day-to-day challenges of the business; replacing top-down leadership practices with lower-level problem solving and decision making; and instituting learning disciplines to create and sustain new behaviors. Their research covered three very diverse organizations: Sears, Roebuck & Company; Royal Dutch Shell; and the United States Army. While very different from one another, the common factor that impaired performance in all three organizations was culture. The researchers identified several predictable indicators of performance that can be used to assess an organization's vital signs. These indicators relate to whether people feel empowered to act, identify with the organization as a whole, manage conflict, and engage in continual learning.

As organizations progress through the six stages of development, their vital signs inevitably wane and they are faced with the crises caused by organizational drift. To counter this tendency, organizations must ensure that every individual understands where the organization is going and is deeply committed to its success. Improvement must become a daily discipline and continual learning a way of being. Learning leaders can serve as the linchpins who help individuals and teams do that. They can play a key role in shifting the focus of organizational change efforts away from incremental change toward an ongoing focus on new learning—engaging everyone in the organizational transformation process.

## New Learning in Practice

Rose Fernandez is in her mid-forties and has worked for the last twenty-five years as a market research manager for a large regional supermarket chain with headquarters in Texas. Caught in a large downsizing, she lost her regular position but was given the opportunity to join a company redeployment pool to see if she could find another position in the organization. Not ready to take early retirement, she realized that her specialized knowledge and expertise could make it difficult to find a new position in the company, especially with the glut of displaced middle managers all scrambling for the few available positions.

One of Rose's hobbies was finding, restoring, and selling old Volkswagen Beetles. She and Tim, a mechanic and co-worker who also lost his job in the downsizing, had been doing this on weekends for several years. When the downsizing hit, they decided to formalize their small VW restoration business. Rose would manage the business and sell the cars that Tim located and restored. They made a good team with Rose's business expertise and Tim's automotive skills. They both continued without success to look for full-time jobs in the organization.

Rose and Tim realized that their little two-person business would not generate enough income to support their respective families. They also realized that each needed to learn more about the other's end of the business to meet prospective car buyers' demands for customization. They went through an intensive hands-on learning process that provided Rose with enough mechanical and auto body knowledge to negotiate with customers. With Rose's tutoring, Tim found he had a flair for business management and decided to pursue a course of study at the local community college.

At about this time, the supermarket's management decided to embark on a regional marketing campaign to entice new customers into their stores. The Southwestern region was experiencing a huge influx of early retirees from other parts of the country, and there was intense competition for this new business among the region's large supermarket chains. Rose and Tim decided to approach their former employer with a promotional idea involving the use of their restored Beetles to carry the company's message to their baby boomer targets, many of whom had once been Beetle owners. The supermarket's management loved the nostalgia theme, and Rose and Tim were off and running.

The Beetle promotion was a great success, and Rose and Tim entered into a long-term contract with the company to develop other marketing promotions involving the use of their fleet of vintage automobiles. Now, several years later, they are the owners of a thriving business with a growing list of enthusiastic clients. Through shared energy and a commitment to learning and collaboration, Rose and Tim are doing what they love and are literally on the road to a successful future.

What enabled Rose and Tim to build a successful new business was the fact that they shared a common vision of the fun and value of restoring old cars and a commitment to developing a working relationship based on interdependence and mutual learning. Neither could have done it alone; it was their relationship and their desire to share in the learning process that made the difference. Rose and Tim used their knowledge, skills, and experience to mentor each other. This is our new mentoring model. Instead of the traditional practice of older individuals imparting their wisdom to younger associates, the new model calls for people at all levels to create reciprocal learning relationships and develop the technical and interpersonal competencies needed to thrive in the new economy. It is through these multiple connections with diverse people that learning happens and people find new meaning and satisfaction in their work.

In today's workplace, everyone is a novice in the sense that every member of the organization must continually acquire new skills and develop new working relationships with diverse groups of people. Managerial mentors are as much new learners as their less-experienced associates. Experienced managers cannot survive on past know-how; they no longer have all the answers, and the collective intelligence of people at all levels of the organization is needed to solve problems with no easy solutions. The added value that experienced managerial mentors contribute is their organizational memory of what has worked in the past, their understanding of the marketplace, and their ability to create a context for change.

## Learning Histories

In an interesting learning experiment on how experience can be a good teacher, an M.I.T. group has developed a tool called the learning history. Designed to address the problem of what they call "undiscussable" issues, the tool is a written narrative of an organizational crisis, such as a product failure, presented in two columns. In one column, the people who participated in, observed, or were affected by the event describe what happened; in the other column, "learned historians," including trained outsiders and knowledgeable insiders, identify recurrent themes in the narrative, raise questions, and bring up the undiscussable issues. The learning history provides the basis for group discussion and learning for those who were involved and others who can learn from it. The learning history could be an excellent tool for you as a learning leader to use in developing learning partnerships. As a managerial mentor and carrier of organizational memory, you are well positioned to help build and disseminate a body of organizational knowledge.

As a learning leader, you are a lot like an airline pilot. While flying over Chicago on the way to Denver, a pilot must simultaneously stay aware of air traffic and changing weather conditions and alter the flight plan as conditions warrant. In other words, to ensure a safe arrival, the pilot must anticipate the future. So it is with you as a managerial mentor. You must take the time to reflect on where your organization is and where it is going. That is no easy task in a turbulent environment, but with a well thought out learning strategy, you have a significant role to play in helping to revitalize your organization.

## Developing New Learning Opportunities

To develop new learning opportunities, you must focus on critical business challenges. There is ample evidence that attempting to initiate revitalization through culture change or structural redesign does not lead to the best results. Instead, you must create individual and team learning opportunities that enhance collaboration, creativity, productivity, and integration.

Your first step in identifying new learning opportunities is to anticipate customer wants and future trends. You need to access multiple sources of information, from the *Wall Street Journal* to trade journals and professional publications. Whether you manage a line or a staff unit, you need to be on the cutting edge. As a learning leader, you must maintain regular contact with your customers and suppliers and network with people both inside and outside of your organization. You must solicit information and dialogue with people in your unit who work directly with customers. A promising learning opportunity will

- Support the organizational vision and promote the unit mission
- Make use of new technology to enhance competitiveness
- Improve quality and service to customers
- Put competitors at a disadvantage
- Add value

Once you have identified a business-driven learning opportunity, it must be translated into a specific action plan that aligns the tasks of everyone in your unit. Organizational revitalization is not just a function of the technical skills of your people but of how well they coordinate with one another in accomplishing value-creating tasks. In other words, task replaces hierarchy as the basis for assigning roles and responsibilities, and knowledge replaces formal authority as the basis for influence.

Beer, Eisenstat, and Spector (1990) studied companies that were revitalized and found that in virtually every case, successful companies focused on critical business issues to motivate change and develop new skills and behaviors. Task alignment, as those researchers defined it, involved a redefinition of work roles, responsibilities, and relationships within an organizational unit to enhance the coordination needed to accomplish critical tasks. By redefining how people work together around core tasks, a cohesive ad hoc team emerges, and the changes brought about by task alignment lead to increased coordination, commitment, and the competence needed for successful revitalization.

### Learning for Task Alignment

The following case, based on a major business problem in a midsize bank, illustrates task alignment. Competitively, the bank was caught in the middle in that it had neither the economies of scale to compete with larger banks on the retail side nor the cost structure and flexibility to compete with smaller banks for institutional business. Management realized that to survive, the organization must drive for operational improvement, not by just reducing costs but by managing costs—that is, figuring out how to perform better without adding to costs. With managing costs identified as the key business challenge, bank unit managers were directed to figure out how to apply the theme to the core tasks in their respective units.

A cross-disciplinary task force of middle managers pinpointed poor coordination between the branches and the operations center as a major cost issue. The task force recommended that a project team collaborate to find a solution. Management approved, and a team was organized. As they worked on the problem, managers and technical staff who traditionally saw themselves as autonomous functionaries and specialists began to perceive themselves as team members on a critical business mission. Later in the chapter, you will learn what the team did to align tasks in order to achieve better cost management, a more collaborative spirit, and a sense of common purpose.

As a learning leader, you can play a critical role in task alignment. You can be instrumental in building individual and team commitment and the competence to manage change. Revitalization is difficult to achieve because it requires new learning and the abandonment of traditional behaviors and work relationships. That threatens people. As a managerial mentor, you can promote the positive side of change and help people understand that the benefits of revitalization far outweigh the risks. You can do that by mobilizing your work unit around tangible business problems that threaten the well-being of everyone in the organization.

Task alignment works because it aligns the organization's ad hoc structure with tangible business problems. Your role is to catalyze the learning process by getting people committed to the need to confront these problems. Unlike organizational change programs built on concepts that people cannot personally relate to, such as abstract vision statements, task alignment enables people to actually experience the change process. They begin to see the personal value of learning skills and behaviors that not only improve organizational performance but give new meaning to their jobs. As a managerial mentor, you simultaneously promote new learning based on competitive realities, contribute to revitalizing your organization, and thereby help to secure your own future.

## Creating Your Learning Plan

Your managerial mentoring plan comprises two components: first, your individual learning plan for acquiring or enhancing the competencies of Collaborator, Innovator, Producer, and Integrator; second, the outline of a task alignment strategy for your work unit. Since most organizations will need to find ways to cope with the challenges of change well into the next century, your job security will depend on your ability to take charge of your own learning and development.

The managerial mentoring model can provide you with a blueprint for how to apply your current competencies in new ways and how to acquire the new competencies you will need to perform effectively in a changing marketplace. The managerial mentoring model is based on the assumption that there is no one right management style, and that to be an effective leader you must possess diverse managerial competencies to cope with competing job demands. A second assumption is

that as an experienced manager you have proven competencies to offer your organization in times of change, and that
you can use that knowledge and experience to bring the best
of your organization's past into the future. As a keeper of
organizational memory, you can play a valuable role in helping less-experienced associates understand what your organization stands for and how it works. To do that, however, you
must first know yourself—what you want to achieve—and
then create a specific learning plan for acquiring or enhancing
the competencies you will need to get there.

As discussed in an earlier section, the 360-degree and
other feedback tools provide an excellent way for you to find
out what you may not know about yourself. Processing 360-
degree feedback to learn how you are perceived by others can
be an invaluable experience if you train people in the process
and use necessary confidentiality safeguards.

An important part of self-awareness is understanding
your strengths and development needs. There are many com-
mercially available self-assessment workbooks for that purpose. To get started, use the questions in Exercise 25 on pages
176—177 to reflect on your current competencies, your
development needs, and what you can do to prepare yourself
to become a learning leader.

As an experienced manager, you should be able to answer
the questions in Exercise 25. If you cannot, you need to do
what was suggested earlier and access multiple sources of
information and network with knowledgeable people inside
and outside of your organization. Remember that as a managerial mentor, especially as an Innovator and Producer, you will
need to be on the cutting edge. Review your answers to
the questions in Exercise 25; then answer the questions in
Exercise 26 on page 177.

## EXERCISE 25: **ASSESSING YOUR MANAGERIAL MENTORING COMPETENCIES**

1. Which of the four learning roles represents your strongest *demonstrated* competency area—that is, which one has contributed the most to your success so far? List the four roles in order, starting with your strongest role.

   a._____   c._____

   b._____   d._____

2. Which of the four learning leader roles represents your *most preferred* way of managing? List the four roles in order of preference.

   a._____   c._____

   b._____   d._____

3. When you rely primarily on your demonstrated or preferred competencies to meet the demands of every managerial situation, they can become weaknesses. How could that become a problem for you in your work, and what specific competencies do you need to strengthen?

4. Given what you know about your work situation, what are the most significant challenges that may lie ahead for you, and what can you do now to prepare yourself?

5. What do you see as your organization's major strategic challenges for the future? Where is it headed and what kinds of changes need to happen for it to make a successful transition into the twenty-first century?

6. Given those strategic challenges, what learning leader roles will be especially important in the successful implementation of the organizational changes you have identified?

7. What specific learning experiences do you need to have to enhance your learning leader competencies and help your organization achieve those change initiatives?

## EXERCISE 26: **YOUR LEARNING LEADER PLAN**

1. As you review your answers to the previous questions, what do you now see as your most critical competency development area as a prospective learning leader?

2. How can you translate that top-priority competency area into a specific learning objective, for example, "I need to learn how to work more collaboratively with my team instead of issuing directives," and how will you monitor your progress?

3. What specific kinds of on- or off-the-job learning experiences—such as serving on a nonprofit board of directors, ad hoc task forces, or performance coaching—might help you acquire the needed learning leader competencies?

One of the most important things you can do is to be proactive in seeking out your own development opportunities. You need to make the development of your learning leader competencies a top priority and create a personal learning agenda based on where your organization is going and how you plan to help it get there. You will need patience and persistence to stay on the cutting edge in a continually changing organizational environment, but you will find that the rewards of becoming a competent and respected learning leader will make it well worth the effort.

## Your Alignment Plan

The second component of your learning plan is an outline of a task alignment strategy for your unit. In the bank case cited earlier, the learning leader started out by holding an off-site meeting to encourage cross-functional relationships among branch managers and technical staff who needed to learn how to coordinate their efforts to solve a critical organization problem. The discussions were self-serving at first, but the group eventually agreed on cost management as a critical business issue that required a collaborative effort. It was the first time that many of the technical and functional unit heads were able to collaborate and dialogue on critical issues that threatened the survival of the organization. As a result, they were able to develop a broader business perspective and find ways to take coordinated action to deal with the threat.

The bank project team realized that they could not move forward without the support of important stakeholders, especially top management, so their next step was to put together a working vision of where they wanted to go and develop a plan for communicating that vision to the stakeholders. Their vision stressed the critical importance of cost management to the bank's survival and the need for people across the organization to commit to and actively participate in the effort. With top management's blessing, the group worked assiduously to develop interdependent relationships among formerly isolated entities. People gradually began to acquire an appreciation for the serious problems caused by poor cooperation and coordination across functional lines. Information began to be more readily shared and people cooperated in solving problems before they developed into major crises. Most important, people in all functions and at all levels throughout the bank began to develop a new understanding of how their own improvement initiatives could impact the bank's bottom line. As other units in the bank began to see the positive results of the team's successful cost management efforts, they were motivated to start their own projects. Thus, a significant performance improvement effort was initiated without changes in the organization chart, and people developed new behaviors by experiencing new learning on the job rather than in the classroom. While there were a few pockets of resistance along the way, the fact that the group followed a specific plan of action enabled them to anticipate and deal with the issues before they became insurmountable barriers.

Beer, Eisenstat, and Spector (1990), whose model was adopted to revitalize the bank, describe a "critical path to renewal." The critical path comprises a number of steps, shown in Exercise 27 on pages 181—182, all of which need to be followed in the indicated sequence.

The alignment process provides an excellent path to unit revitalization. Task alignment is a continuing process, and as a learning leader, you can help build the necessary coordinating bridges to make sure it happens. Your organizational knowledge and experience give you the broad perspective needed to mentor such efforts. By helping people focus on real business problems, you can build a commitment to change and a community of learners.

## EXERCISE 27: **YOUR ALIGNMENT PLAN**

In your role as a learning leader, answer each of the following questions to develop an alignment plan for your work unit:

1.  Who are your key stakeholders and what can you do to get them to support you in diagnosing critical problems that impact your unit's performance and could threaten your ability to get the job done now or in the future? Are there pockets of dissatisfaction or an awareness of the need for change?

2.  What steps can you take to get the people in your unit involved in the creation of a tangible vision of the future, including where you need to go in the future and what specific changes in behavior will be needed to realize that vision?

3.  What kinds of resistance can you anticipate, and what type of process can you create to get people to come to their own realization of the need for change (for example, a process that would help people identify the need for team-building training)?

EXERCISE 27: **YOUR ALIGNMENT PLAN** (cont'd)

4. What specific things can you learn or change to ensure that you do not dictate the solution-finding process, such as developing your Facilitating competency?

5. What are some formal structural and systems changes that you anticipate might be needed to support the new behaviors that people identify? Will it be possible for you to make them if necessary?

6. What types of monitoring procedures can you set up to ensure that problems that may arise during the process—such as power struggles—are addressed and midcourse corrections are made?

CHAPTER NINE

# Learning Organizations as Communities of Purpose

MANAGERIAL MENTORS USE THEIR knowledge and experience to grow and change and to help others do the same. They act as teachers and stewards, encouraging people to continually acquire the new skills they need to help their organizations thrive in a new era. Peter Senge (1990), who first promoted the concept of the learning organization in *The Fifth Discipline*, goes beyond the traditional definition of learning as an act of acquiring information; he sees learning as a process of individual change that in turn enables people to develop a special level of personal mastery that enables them to accomplish things that are really important to them. He says, "in effect, they approach their life as an artist would approach a work of art. They do that by becoming committed to their own lifelong learning" (p. 7).

It is not easy to become a managerial mentor in a learning organization. The Collaborator, Innovator, Producer, and

Integrator role competencies are necessary but not sufficient for effective learning leadership. By way of analogy, one cannot become an Olympic figure skater without first acquiring the basic skating skills. Once these skills are acquired, the focus must shift from the skill components to the whole performance. To become an Olympic champion, the skater must combine and apply all the skill components to achieve performance excellence.

As in skating, learning leadership requires more than the acquisition of a set of managerial mentoring competencies; these competencies are necessary but not sufficient. Learning leadership calls for what Peter Vaill (1996) describes as learning as a way of being. To paraphrase his words, learning leadership is not learned; learning leadership *is* learning and, as such, is an ongoing process. This is very different from the traditional view of managerial learning as the acquisition of individual competencies to solve problems and control outcomes. Learning leadership calls for a radically new way of thinking and being with others. It places more emphasis on the joint exploration of individual assumptions and beliefs to surface diverse perspectives on key issues. The focus is on processes that foster mutual understanding, continual learning, and the creation of communities of inquiry. By encouraging people to make explicit their assumptions on important organizational issues, such as emerging marketplaces and competitive threats, managerial mentors help defuse the defensiveness and the fear of being wrong that typically occur in traditional command-and-control settings.

As organizations have come to realize that learning will be their key to survival, they have begun to preach empowerment and risk taking, frequently with disappointing results. Given survivor anxiety in an era of continued downsizing, people are extremely reluctant to experiment with new ways. If you think of yourself as a circus high-wire performer struggling to get across a swaying tightrope, the last thing you need when you cannot afford to make a mistake is someone yelling at you to try a new move. That is what it feels like to organizational survivors when managers exhort them to challenge the status quo. If organizations want people to step out on tightropes, they must first provide safety nets in the form of learning leaders who will support people in taking risks and experimenting with new ways.

In many organizations today, there are no safety nets. The old social compact, with its traditions and rules, is rapidly disappearing, and organizations are struggling to find new ways to rebuild trust and commitment. Organizational leaders, realizing that people are disillusioned and distrustful, are casting about for solutions, practicing what some corporate cynics call management by best-seller. What these leaders fail to realize is that trust and commitment flow from principles-based leadership, not new tools and techniques. The power to move an organization ultimately comes from its people, and only by working with those people to develop shared values and a renewed sense of purpose will learning leaders be able to help their organizations move into a new era.

## Leading with a Purpose

Most people want meaningful work. If organizations could understand that, they would save the millions of dollars they now spend on programs about how to motivate people. People will be self-motivated when they are doing something they believe in. When people share a commitment to the achievement of a compelling goal, extraordinary things happen, as illustrated by the 1969 NASA moon landing eight years after John Kennedy first issued his challenge to achieve that goal by the end of the decade.

It has been predicted that in the twenty-first century, most people will extend their work lives to the age of seventy-five. One does not have to look very far today to see that work is no longer a source of meaning and fulfillment for many people. If people are going to work longer, managerial mentors must lead the way in helping them create more meaningful work. There is an old parable about three bricklayers who were asked by a passerby to explain what they were doing. The first worker said, "I am laying bricks." The second replied, "I am feeding my family by laying bricks." The third answered, "I am laying bricks to construct a cathedral to serve the Lord." It is your challenge as a learning leader to help the people in your work unit find and commit to a shared purpose they believe in. If your organization as a whole has a clear, overarching purpose that people already relate to, your task in working with them to translate that broad purpose into a compelling unit mission is much easier.

One of the best living examples of an organization with purpose is the ServiceMaster Company. The organization's purpose is expressed in its company credo: "We serve." Recognized by *Fortune* magazine over the last ten years as the number-one service company among the Fortune 500, ServiceMaster's belief in service is the foundation for building its common purpose. It gives ServiceMaster a reason for being and helps its people focus their efforts, find meaning in their work, and become part of something greater than themselves. ServiceMaster sees itself as being in the learning business, based on its assumption that the best way to deliver high-quality service is to unleash people's potential to fulfill themselves. Managers are expected to be learning leaders. Service-Master CEO C. William Pollard (1996) believes that every-one in the organization should be a teacher/learner and that people who do not want to take the time to teach do not belong at ServiceMaster. For the people at ServiceMaster, work is more than a job or a means of earning a living. According to Pollard, it is a mission—a way of life.

By personally committing to and championing Service-Master's common purpose and modeling it in everything that he says and does, CEO Pollard serves as a true learning leader. He sees his role as involving more than what people do on the job. He is concerned about what they are becoming as whole people and how their work environment is con-tributing to the process. He quotes the founder of Service-Master as saying, "If you don't live it, you don't believe it."

The shared purpose that is created in a learning organiza-tion is very different from the loyalist ethic of the past. For the employees of traditional organizations, putting in time and effort meant that even in down times, the organization had an obligation to provide them with job security. With the advent of corporate downsizing, those loyalists were infuriated when their long-standing social compact was violated. In the learn-ing organization, the social compact is an ongoing, negotiated process based on open communication between the parties about the continuing value of the relationship. The fact that an individual has been a loyal worker for twenty-five years is not what counts; what counts is the contribution that the individual continually makes to the organization. Both parties must feel that the relationship is productive and that there is a joint commitment to reaching an accommodation of purpose.

As a managerial mentor, you are an important linchpin in the ongoing negotiation between individuals and the organization. You must help survivors stuck in the old loyalty ethic learn that in a new era, doing one's job is not enough. To thrive in the future, they must do more than their jobs and continually seek and find new ways to enhance their contribution to the achievement of the mission.

## Learning to Serve

It is not possible to talk about a learning organization without talking about a new kind of leadership. Over twenty-five years ago, an AT&T executive named Robert Greenleaf articulated a vision of what he called "servant-leadership." Greenleaf's thesis was that a true leader is one who leads by empowering others to reach their full potential. He viewed the ideal leader as an individual who transforms and integrates an organization, a steward with a commitment to building communities of purpose. As traditional leadership models are giving way to a newer model based on teamwork, community, and personal growth, interest in Greenleaf's (1977) servant-leadership concept is reaching an all-time high. In *Fortune* magazine, Walter Kiechel (1992) compared servant-leadership to the Japanese consensus-building process in which everyone's view is solicited but people understand that their own point of view may not necessarily prevail. Kiechel adds that while this approach takes a lot of time up front, things really begin to happen once people reach consensus.

Greenleaf's servant-leaders have much in common with learning leaders. Both put top priority on serving people—colleagues, customers, and other stakeholders—and sharing decision-making power. Greenleaf makes a clear distinction between two extreme types of leadership. The first type, traditional command-and-control leadership, is based on a high need for power and uses coercion to get things done. The second type, servant-leadership, relies on persuasion rather than coercion and stems from a motivation to serve others. Greenleaf had a strong belief that individuals can and do make a difference, even in a high-technology world.

Changes in technology, information, and communications are having a dramatic impact on the way organizations do their work. One outcome is the emergence of the virtual organization, where organizations are no longer defined by their physical assets or ownership. In the virtual organization, the primary source of competitive advantage will be the shared commitment to a compelling mission by diverse, self-directed people working in geographically distant locations. Business philosopher Charles Handy (1997) wrote: "Power, in the new organizations, comes from relationships, not from structures. Those who have established reputations acquire authority which was not handed down from above; those who are open to others create positive energy around themselves, energy which did not exist before" (p. 379).

Greenleaf's model of the servant-leader, based on persuasion and caring for the growth and development of others, is the way to manage the virtual organizations of the coming century. It also parallels the personal qualities of the learning leader.

Larry C. Spears (1995) of the Robert K. Greenleaf Center for Servant-Leadership has identified ten characteristics of the servant-leader. Notice how closely these characteristics resemble the competencies of the managerial mentor.

1. *Listening.* Servant-leaders listen to try to identify the will of a group and help it articulate that will. They couple listening with personal reflection and a commitment to deeply listening to others.

2. *Empathy.* Servant-leaders assume that people have good intentions and do not reject them as people even when they behave or perform poorly. They try to understand and recognize people for their special qualities.

3. *Healing.* Servant-leaders are committed to healing themselves and others. In downsized organizations, they support disaffected survivors to help them become whole again.

4. *Awareness.* Servant-leaders strive for self-awareness. They trust awareness as a way of understanding issues relating to ethics and values.

5. *Persuasion.* Servant-leaders rely on persuasion rather than role power to make decisions. They try to build group consensus and reject coercion.

6. *Conceptualization.* Servant-leaders are practical visionaries. They try to achieve a workable balance between conceptual thinking and task-focused action.

7. *Foresight.* Servant-leaders try to integrate past learning, current realities, and probable outcomes. They use intuition to try to anticipate the likely consequences of a particular course of action.

8. *Stewardship.* Servant-leaders are fully committed to serving the needs of others. They believe that they have a responsibility to hold their organizations in trust for the greater good of others.

9. *Commitment to the Growth of Others.* Servant-leaders value people for more than their work contribution. They are firmly committed to helping people achieve their full potential and feel

responsible for nurturing their personal, professional, and spiritual growth. Their commitment is demonstrated in their efforts to support people affected by corporate downsizing.

10. *Building Community.* Servant-leaders work to restore a sense of community in large, impersonal organizations. They believe that communities play an important role in shaping people's lives and try to show the way through their own actions.

Servant-leadership is a viable business model, and diverse organizations—for example, ServiceMaster, AT&T Consumer Products Education, The Toro Company, and the Herman Miller Company—use it as part of their corporate philosophy. Servant-leadership materials are used in the corporate education programs in hundreds of organizations, and leaders from around the world attend the annual conference of the Robert K. Greenleaf Center for Servant-Leadership.

Some people, including women and people of color, take exception to the use of the word *servant* because of its negative connotation, and it often takes time and reflection on their part to understand the positive use of the word. In fact, the inherent paradox in the pairing of *servant* and *leadership* often fosters a new awareness that, in reality, servant-leaders are modeling democracy by serving those who are led rather than expecting to be served by them.

Most critics of servant-leadership dislike the idea of the leader listening, interpreting the will of the group, expressing that will, and trying to further it. They contend that listening takes too much time and that, anyway, most people want a plan and want the leader to set the direction. Advocates of servant-leadership acknowledge that listening may take more time up front, but that once a consensus is forged, things get implemented fast. TDIndustries, a multimillion-dollar-a-year contracting firm in Dallas, has used servant-leadership to train its managers for over two decades. Its CEO, Jack Lowe Jr., says, with tongue in cheek, "It sounds a little like the quality movement, doesn't it?"

The servant-leadership model provides managerial mentors with a new philosophical framework for working as Collaborators, Innovators, Producers, and Integrators. It is true that the practice of servant-leadership calls for a different approach to time management. Focusing on people becomes more important than just getting through a managerial to-do list as quickly as possible. Servant-leaders work with task forces to help people learn how to ask the right questions and discover answers that the whole team can commit to; they encourage self-initiated work projects and offer supportive coaching; they mentor others on how to get innovative ideas through the system. Servant-leadership sounds like the right work for the twenty-first-century learning leader. As a learning leader, you bring your own vision to the group, but you also realize that everyone else has his or her own personal vision. Through your openness and willingness to listen and speak in a way that engages people, a shared vision can emerge, and that shared vision is essential to the creation of a true learning organization.

If servant-leadership sounds unduly idealistic for a competitive, global marketplace, it is useful to keep in mind that concern for the spirit is a major issue in today's business world. Mass layoffs through downsizing have caused millions of people to reexamine their lives and lose their trust in established institutions. Members of diverse groups are demanding greater participation and more caring workplaces. Middle-aged workaholics are seeking more balanced lifestyles and more meaningful work. Given the fallout from the greed of the eighties, it may be that Greenleaf's thesis of uplifting the human spirit is the best way to restore meaning and value to the marketplace.

## Becoming a Servant-Leader

In the edited collection *Reflections on Leadership*, by Larry Spears (1995), the executive director of the Greenleaf Center for Servant-Leadership, a number of prominent management leaders explore the servant-leadership concept in such areas as team building, corporate risk taking, and spirit in the workplace. This book provides an excellent introduction to Robert Greenleaf's thinking and demonstrates the power of his ideas on the nature of leadership.

The questions in Exercise 28 on page 194 will help you think about the relevance of servant-leadership for you as a managerial mentor.

## Building Communities of Purpose

Developing a new way of thinking and being has profound implications for the creation of communities of purpose. Futurists talk about the concept of scientific float, meaning the time between the invention of a new technology and its widespread application. While it took decades for the automobile to gain universal acceptance and years for radio and television to do the same, with the use of microchips new devices are in use throughout the world in a matter of days. Today, everything is constantly changing, and the float time between past and future is disappearing, with one important exception: Organizational float is still much in evidence in

## EXERCISE 28: **YOU AND SERVANT-LEADERSHIP**

1. As you think about the ten characteristics of the servant-leader described earlier in the chapter, which ones have particular meaning for you as a learning leader and why?

2. What characteristics of servant-leadership currently exist in your organization and how are they manifested?

3. When, either inside or outside of your organization, have you experienced team decision making in action, and how did you feel about the process?

4. In what ways could the practice of servant-leadership help your organization make a successful transition into the twenty-first century?

that the Newtonian machine metaphor, with its emphasis on hierarchical command and control, is still the concept that drives many organizations.

New information technology is having a profound impact on society as organizations in every sector are coming to the realization that the old hierarchical forms, with their concentration of power and wealth, are no longer viable and that new concepts of organization, based on shared power and control, are needed. Managerial expertise must shift from the outdated Industrial Age concept of control, uniformity, and efficiency to a new understanding of how to cope with variability, complexity, and change.

If you were to ask most managers today what they see as their prime responsibility, you might get a variety of responses, but chances are that most will still reflect the traditional, downward view of the manager as one who has authority over the work of others. That is wrong. The prime responsibility of managers as learning leaders in today's organizations is first to manage themselves, and second to use their mentoring competencies to support, influence, and help others learn how to manage themselves. In that way, managerial control over others becomes an anachronism, and responsible, self-motivated people can build communities of purpose. Only when people in an organization feel trusted and connected as partners in learning can a high level of community exist.

Fortunately, there are a number of organizations in existence that see themselves as communities. An example is Herman Miller, Inc., whose leader, Max De Pree, models the qualities of a servant-leader. This innovative furniture manufacturer has regularly been included among the top twenty-five firms on *Fortune's* list of the most-admired companies in the

United States. De Pree believes that leaders owe a covenant to the people who comprise their organizations and that those covenants bind people together and enable them to flourish by meeting the needs of one another. In the foreword to De Pree's *Leadership Is an Art*, business professor James O'Toole (1989) of the University of California made the following observations about De Pree's leadership role at Herman Miller: "Max's excellence as a leader was manifested in the productive spirit of self-management that I found in every Herman Miller employee—worker or manager—with whom I spoke. . . . I discovered that Max practiced what he preached, but so did the people who worked for him—the people he served" (pp. xxii—xxiii).

Max De Pree and such other outstanding organizational leaders as Frances Hesselbein, former CEO of the Girl Scouts of America, have created true organizational communities based on common purpose and shared values. They have created space for learning at all levels of the organization and have put control in the hands of local line leaders.

Transforming traditional hierarchies into communities of purpose presents learning leaders with a formidable challenge. Building community is not a fast track to profitability. It takes courage to persist in the face of resistance and requires a strong commitment to the long-term value to the organization of shared vision, teamwork, and open communication. Learning leaders must believe that helping people find new meaning and purpose in their work will ultimately lead to enhanced performance.

Building learning communities does not depend on the total abandonment of all hierarchical structures. Managerial mentors who listen, support, and serve others in hierarchies will be more successful community builders than self-centered, free-agent managers in horizontal structures. *Knowing about* community and *building* community are different things, and community building is not a program. Building community is something that is both a process and a way of being, and only by working together in that process can people learn to be a community.

Some organizational leaders question the realism of community building in the rough-and-tumble downsizing era. In intensely competitive times, who has time to worry about issues of the spirit? Management guru Tom Peters decries the New Age tendency to confuse workplace spirit with spirituality. While he has long championed the importance of vision, values, and spirit, Peters fears that when organizations go overboard on spirituality and begin to act more like religious institutions, they are treading on dangerous ground.

Lee and Zemke (1995, p. 108) cite the warnings of such organizational experts as Harry Levinson that trying to implement community-building principles in take-charge cultures will not work. Levinson contends that the image of manager-as-workplace-messiah ignores the issue of accountability and fails to acknowledge the existence of aggressive impulses in people. Like Peters, Levinson believes that spiritual talk should be kept out of the workplace.

Those who support the search for spirit in the workplace contend that they are not trying to mix business and religion but are trying to lead with values that give people meaning and a reason to want to go to work every day. These are the managerial mentors who see themselves as learning partners who collaborate with others in setting and achieving high-performance goals. Successful community building is not about New Age spiritualism, it is about believing in a deeply valued organizational purpose and a shared commitment to productive outcomes. The higher road may not be the expressway, but it may turn out to be the best route to the next century.

## The Twenty-First Century Learning Community

An organization that wants to move successfully into the twenty-first century must become a generative learning community. Organizational learning communities facilitate the learning of all of their members and continually transform themselves. Organizational transformation calls for more than helping people do things better by improving their work processes and relationships; it means finding new and different ways of working in uncharted territory where change is the norm and where there are no experts to provide answers. It means that people at all organizational levels, not just learning leaders, must develop the new competencies they need to cope with unfamiliar and unpredictable work environments.

A learning community is a group of people united by a common purpose who work together to achieve what no one individual could accomplish alone. Because it is a way of being more than a way of doing, it is not possible to draw an organizational chart of a learning community. A learning community does not have to be an entire organization; as a managerial mentor, you can develop a learning community in your organizational unit by fostering a developmental climate based on co-learning and mutual support.

The rebirth of a spirit of community in the workplace should be a priority concern of all learning leaders. The workplace is becoming a kind of surrogate family for many people, yet what one finds in many organizations is people cloistered

198

in cubicles with little or no opportunity for direct interaction. In *In the Age of the Smart Machine,* Harvard professor Shoshana Zuboff (1988) paints a grim picture of how new office technology can isolate people: "Jobs which had once allowed . . . interpersonal exchange and collaboration now required . . . routine interaction with a machine. Jobs that had once required their voices now insisted they be mute. Jobs that had . . . used at least some small measure of their person-hood now emphasized their least differentiated . . . capacities" (p. 141).

Contrast that distressing picture with the stories of the engineers who collaborated in the design of Apple's Macintosh computer. These engineers felt so strongly about their organization's contribution to society that they printed all of their names inside of each new computer. In its early days, that community spirit contributed significantly to Apple's spectacular success.

In the current Information Age, where people are geographically dispersed, a renewed sense of community that contributes to increased cooperation across organizational boundaries is even more important. In a highly networked marketplace, people will cooperate when they feel like members of the same organization who share a common purpose. To achieve productivity in the Information Age, organizations need people whose sense of community will lead them to break down traditional bureaucratic barriers and share knowledge across organizational boundaries. In the networked organizations of the coming century, shared values provide a better basis for community spirit than hierarchical chains of command.

Community spirit is not just a matter of believing in an organization's purpose and mission; it also requires an understanding of how that organization works. When people understand how their day-to-day actions affect organizational outcomes, they learn to think and act like owners. A promising new concept designed to increase people's understanding of a business is called *open-book management.* The simple underlying premise of this approach is that by teaching people about a business and giving them a chance to act on that knowledge, they will see their work as more than just a job. Furthermore, they will develop a sense of community spirit based on the belief that they are all in that business together and are accountable to one another for making sure that it succeeds. When people know everything that is happening in the business, there are no surprises; understanding builds trust. Community spirit emerges from common rather than parochial goals, and while special interests do not disappear, they are perceived differently. For example, in unionized companies, the traditional adversarial relationship between unions and management shifts from a zero-sum game of how to divide up the existing pie to a discussion of how to create a larger pie. Open-book management facilitates productive innovation in all aspects of the business and builds continual learning into the organization. Open-book organizations, in other words, become true learning organizations.

John Case (1995) says in *Open-Book Management* that its principles and practices can be summarized in a few words: treat people like adults. Case describes open-book management as a business system based on four principles:

1. Get information to people about what they need to know to do their jobs effectively *and* how their unit or the organization as a whole is doing.

2. Teach people business literacy in the form of fundamental financial data about the business and how to understand and use it.

3. Show people how their work affects the unit's or the organization's bottom line, and empower them to be responsible and accountable for their own decisions and numbers.

4. Give everyone a stake in the business, and reward them accordingly for the part they play in the company's success or failure.

While Case's examples of open-book management come from the business sector, the principles can be applied in nonprofit and government organizations. Case points out that such traditionally nonprofit organizations as hospitals and universities are really double—bottom line organizations: As organizations, they must make sure that their revenues exceed their expenses, but their people do not think of themselves as being in the business of making money and typically do not know how to measure the cost of activities. While nonprofit organizations must pay primary attention to their missions, they can also take responsibility for costs, revenues, and budgets in the interest of running things more efficiently.

In the current managed health care environment, medical professionals and hospital personnel express anger and frustration over what they view as a bottom-line emphasis at the expense of quality patient care. They fear layoffs, and morale suffers. In these changing times, all nonprofit organizations, including hospitals, will face stiffer competition, leaner budgets, and an increasingly complex environment. In the past, hospitals could spend whatever they could raise and then mount a new fundraising campaign. That is no longer the case, and the hospitals and other nonprofit organizations that learn how to operate more efficiently while still pursuing their worthy missions will be those that survive and provide the best service.

Open-book management is not just one more packaged business program. It works better than such programs as team building and empowerment because it assumes that to have a real stake in things, people must understand the numbers. With that understanding, they can become both independent and interdependent decision makers.

Critics of open-book management complain that it is too bottom line — focused and exacerbates what is already wrong with American business. By taking a closer look, however, they will see that the practice of open-book management is not incompatible with such "soft" concepts as servant-leadership. Herman Miller, Inc., cited earlier in this chapter as a proponent of servant-leadership, also employs management practices that directly parallel open-book management. Nearly a quarter of the company is owned by directors or people on the payroll, and bonuses are pegged to key financial and operational targets. Every month all six thousand Herman Miller employees receive videos with current information about the state of the business.

Open-book management can contribute to organizational transformation. It provides a way of thinking that gets people working cooperatively toward shared goals. It helps build a continual learning mind-set into the organization. People begin to think about their jobs differently and get excited by new challenges. In other words, people become active players in the game, not just automatons who show up for work and put in time.

Just as there is no one "right" management approach to every situation, there is no one "right" approach to organizational community building. Seemingly incompatible sets of values and beliefs about how to build community spirit— such as servant-leadership and open-book management—can be integrated in ways that build positive relationships and establish a clear direction for the achievement of performance excellence.

## The New Managerial Mentor

Learning leaders are sorely needed to guide downsized organizations back to health and productivity. Organizations need emotionally intelligent managers who will help people develop the competencies and commitment to work together in the new "knowledge economy." To become learning leaders, managers must first gain full competence in each of the four managerial mentoring roles: Collaborator, Innovator, Producer, and Integrator.

Becoming a learning leader starts with self-knowledge. You must be clear on the principles and values that really matter to you and how you will reflect them in your everyday words and actions. As a managerial mentor, you must bridge the differences among people and foster the talents of diverse groups to meet the competing demands of the Information Age. Your goal as a learning leader must be to help build flexible, mature teams of people who can continually reinvent themselves to accommodate organizational change. In chaotic and complex times, no individual learning leader or team of learning leaders can capitalize on every opportunity or meet every threat. Therefore, you must create a culture of learning leaders at all levels who can serve as internal change agents to facilitate change.

The next century will present you as a learning leader with new and exciting challenges. You cannot reengineer people's commitment. You must build commitment one relationship at a time by ensuring that every individual feels listened to, respected, and valued for his or her contribution to a shared purpose. A new kind of organizational community is emerging—the learning organization of the managerial mentor—and you can help lead the way.

# References

Argyris, C. "Teaching Smart People How to Learn." *Harvard Business Review*, May—June 1991.

Aubrey, R., and Cohen, C. *Working Wisdom.* San Francisco: Jossey-Bass, 1995.

Baker, W. *Networking Smart.* New York: McGraw-Hill, 1994.

Beer, M., Eisenstat, R., and Spector, B. *The Critical Path to Corporate Renewal.* Boston: Harvard Business School Press, 1990.

Bennis, W. *Organizing Genius: The Secrets of Creative Collaboration.* Reading, Mass.: Addison-Wesley, 1997.

Bennis, W., Benne, K., and Chin, R. *The Planning of Change.* New York: Holt, Rinehart and Winston, 1961.

Bennis, W., and Goldsmith, J. *Learning to Lead.* Reading, Mass.: Addison-Wesley, 1994.

Binney, G., and Williams, C. *Leaning into the Future.* London: Nicholas Brealey, 1995.

Block, P. *The Empowered Manager: Positive Political Skills at Work.* San Francisco: Jossey-Bass, 1987.

Bridges, W. *JobShift.* Reading, Mass.: Addison-Wesley, 1994.

Case, J. *Open-Book Management.* New York: HarperCollins, 1995.

Cooper, R. *Executive EQ.* New York: Grosset/Putnam, 1996.

Drucker, P. *Managing for the Future: The 1990s and Beyond.* New York: Penguin-Putnam, 1993.

Drucker, P. "Toward the New Organization." In Hesselbein, F., Goldsmith, M., and Beckhard, R. (eds.), *The Organization of the Future.* San Francisco: Jossey-Bass, 1997.

Dyson, E. "So Many Ideas, So Few Companies." *The New York Times*, February 15, 1998.

Fournies, F. *Coaching for Improved Work Performance.* New York: McGraw-Hill, 1987.

Fritz, R. *Creating.* New York: Fawcett-Columbine, 1991.

Greenleaf, R. *Servant-Leadership.* Mahwah, N.J.: Paulist Press, 1977.

Hall, D., and Associates. *The Career Is Dead—Long Live the Career.* San Francisco: Jossey-Bass, 1994.

Hammer, M., and Champy, J. *Reengineering the Corporation.* New York: HarperCollins, 1993.

Handy, C. *The Age of Paradox.* Boston: Harvard Business School Press, 1994.

Handy, C. "Unimagined Futures." In Hesselbein, F., Goldsmith, M., and Beckhard, R. (eds.), *The Organization of the Future.* San Francisco: Jossey-Bass, 1997.

Handy, C. *The Hungry Spirit.* New York: Broadway Books, 1998.

Heckscher, C. *White Collar Blues.* New York: Basic Books, 1995.

Helgesen, S. *The Web of Inclusion.* New York: Doubleday/Currency, 1995.

Huang, C., and Lynch, J. *Mentoring.* New York: HarperCollins, 1995.

Isaacs, W. "Taking Flight: Dialogue, Collective Thinking and Organizational Learning." *Organizational Dynamics,* Fall 1993.

Kanter, R. M. *The Change Masters.* New York: Simon & Schuster, 1983.

Kanter, R. M. *World Class: Thriving Locally in the Global Economy.* New York: Simon & Schuster, 1995.

Katzenbach, J. R., and the RCL Team. *Real Change Leaders.* New York: Times Business Random House, 1995.

Kelley, R., and Caplan, J. "How Bell Labs Creates Star Performers." *Harvard Business Review,* July—August 1993.

Kiechel, W. "The Leader as Servant." *Fortune,* May 1992.

Kotter, J. *The General Managers.* New York: Free Press, 1982.

Lawrence, P., and Lorsch, J. *Organization and Environment.* Boston: Harvard Business School Press, 1986 (1967).

Lee, C., and Zemke, R. In Spears, L. (ed.) *Reflections on Leadership.* New York: Wiley, 1995.

Lipnack, J., and Stamps, J. *The Age of the Network.* New York: Wiley, 1994.

Lombardi, V. *Coaching for Teamwork: Winning Concepts for Business in the Twenty-First Century.* Reinforcement Press, 1995.

Maccoby, M. *Why Work.* New York: Simon & Schuster, 1988.

Murphy, K. "Generative Coaching: A Surprising Learning Odyssey." In Chawla, S., and Renesch, J., *Learning Organizations.* Portland, Ore.: Productivity Press, 1995.

Noer, D. *Healing the Wounds.* San Francisco: Jossey-Bass, 1993.

Noer, D. *Breaking Free.* San Francisco: Jossey-Bass, 1997.

O'Brien, T. "Encourage Wild Ideas." *Fast Company,* Special Collectors Edition, Vol. 1, 1996.

O'Toole, J. "History, Leadership, and a Vision of Corporate Life." In De Pree, M., *Leadership Is an Art.* New York: Dell, 1989.

Pascale, R., Millemann, M., and Gioga, L. "Changing the Way We Change." *Harvard Business Review,* November—December 1997.

Pedler, M., Burgoyne, J., and Boydell, T. *The Learning Company.* New York: McGraw-Hill, 1991.

Peters, T. "The Brand Called You." *Fast Company,* August—September 1997.

Peters, T., and Waterman, R. *In Search of Excellence: Lessons from America's Best-Run Companies.* New York: HarperCollins, 1982.

Pitcher, P. *The Drama of Leadership.* New York: Wiley, 1997.

Pollard, W. *The Soul of the Firm.* New York: HarperCollins, 1996.

Quinn, R. *Deep Change.* San Francisco: Jossey-Bass, 1996.

Robbins, R., and Finley, M. *Why Change Doesn't Work.* Princeton, N.J.: Peterson's/Pacesetter, 1996.

Rogers, C. *On Becoming a Person.* Boston: Houghton Mifflin, 1961.

Ross, R. "Moments of Awareness." In Senge, P. et al., *The Fifth Discipline Handbook.* New York: Doubleday, 1994.

Schultz, H., and Yang, D. *Pour Your Heart into It: How Starbucks Built a Company One Cup at a Time.* Winnipeg, Manitoba: Hyperion, 1997.

Senge, P. *The Fifth Discipline.* New York: Doubleday/Currency, 1990a.

Senge, P. "The Leaders' New Work." *Sloan Management Review,* 1990b.

Senge, P., Roberts, C., Ross, R., Smith, B., and Kleiner, A. *The Fifth Discipline Handbook.* New York: Doubleday, 1994.

Spears, L. "What Is Servant-Leadership?" In Spears, L. (ed.), *Reflections on Leadership.* New York: Wiley, 1995.

Stewart, R. *Choices for the Manager.* Upper Saddle River, N.J.: Prentice-Hall, 1982.

Tichy, N. *The Leadership Engine.* New York: HarperCollins, 1997.

Vaill, P. *Managing as a Performing Art.* San Francisco: Jossey-Bass, 1989.

Vaill, P. *Learning as a Way of Being.* San Francisco: Jossey-Bass, 1996.

Van Velsor, E., and Leslie, J. B. *Feedback to Managers* (Vols. I & II). Greensboro, NC: Center for Creative Leadership, 1991.

White, R., Hodgson, P., and Crainer, S. *The Future of Leadership.* London: Pitman, 1996.

Zaleznik, A. "Managers and Leaders: Are They Different?" *Harvard Business Review,* May—June 1997.

Zaleznik, A. "Real Work." *Harvard Business Review,* November—December 1997.

Zuboff, S. *In the Age of the Smart Machine.* New York: HarperCollins, 1988.

# Index

coalition building. *See* Championing competency

Cohen, C., xiii-xiv

co-learning: barriers to, 64-65; for corporate survivors, 56-57; in relationships, 19-22, 169; *See also* Coaching competency

Collaborator role, 30-32, 47-49; in action, 72-74, 144; Coaching competency in, 56-62, 63, 132; developing effectiveness in, 74-76; Dialoguing competency in, 62-71, 132; Facilitating competency in, 49-55, 132; and role preference inventory, 35-42

communication: Bridging competency for, 142-143; and Facilitating competency, 49-54; *See also* listening

communities of purpose, 183-185; building, xi, xiii, 77, 193-198; leading with purpose in, 185-188; servant-leadership in, 188-193, 194; in the twenty-first century, xi, 198-204; *See also* learning organizations

competencies, 16, 28; assessing, 175-177; of Collaborator role, 30-32; defined, 29; of Innovator role, 30-32, 33; of Integrator role, 30-32, 34; model of, 29-32; and plan for individual learning, 174-178; of Producer role, 30-32, 33-34; and role preference inventory, 35-41; *See also under specific roles*

consensus building, 64, 188

constraints, defined, 13-14

contracts, psychological, traditional vs. new, 20-22, 47-48

Cooper, R., 49-50; *Executive EQ,* 48-49

craftsmen (type of leader), 27-28

Crainer, S., *The Future of Leadership,* 16

*Creating* (Fritz), 83

creative tension, defined, 83

creativity, 28; and Visioning competency, 81, 85-86; *See also* Innovator role

customer satisfaction, 148, 165; Bridging competency for, 143, 144-145; as foundation for improvements, 137-138, 143, 144-145; learning opportunities developed for, 171-174; measuring, 119-120

debate, 66, 67, 68

decision making, 120-121

*Deep Change* (Quinn), 25-26, 30

deep listening, 52, 53

demands, defined, 13-14

De Pree, M., 195-196; *Leadership Is an Art,* 196

design, organizational. *See* Organizing competency

development exercises: for Bridging competency, 145-147; for Championing competency, 94-96; for Coaching competency, 62, 63; for Collaborator role, 75, 76; for Dialoguing competency, 70-71; for Diffusing competency, 100-101; for Facilitating competency, 55; for Improving competency, 140-142; for Improvising competency, 118-119; for Innovator role, 103, 104; for Integrator role, 150-152; for Measuring competency, 122-123; for Organizing competency, 136-137; for Producer role, 106, 124-127; for Targeting competency, 113; for Visioning competency, 83, 85-88, 89

dialogue, 23, 49, 64, 91; defined, 66; ground rules for, 50, 67, 68

Dialoguing competency, 62-65; in action, 65-68; assessing, 68-69; developing, 70-71

Diffusing competency, 96-97; in action, 97-98; assessing, 98-99; developing, 100-101

discovery learning, 114

downsizing: and emotions in the workplace, 47-49, 50-52; in life cycle of organizations, 164-165; and loyalty ethic, x-xi, 47-48, 187-188; and survival as focus, ix, x, 21, 107, 149; *See also* survivor anxiety

*Drama of Leadership, The* (Pitcher), 27

Drucker, P., *Managing for the Future,* 159; "Toward the New Organization," 77

Dyson, E., "So Many Ideas, So Few Companies," 108

EDS, 114

Educational Testing Service, 107

Innovator role *(continued)*
  competency in, 88-96, 132; Coaching
  competency in, 60; developing effectiveness in, 103-104; Diffusing competency in, 96-101, 132; and role preference inventory, 35-41; Visioning competency in, 80-88, 89, 132
*In Search of Excellence* (Peters and Waterman), 130
Integrator role, 12, 30-32, 34, 129-131;
  in action, 85, 148-149; Bridging
  competency in, 142-148; developing
  effectiveness in, 150-152; Improving
  competency in, 137-142; Organizing
  competency in, 132-137; and role
  preference inventory, 35-41
Intel, 32, 162
interdependence, xiii, 22, 144; and relational model, 19-20, 169
Isaacs, W., "Taking Flight," 62-64

jobs: as boxes of activity, 12-14, 15, 29,
  132; performance on, 105-108, 155;
  security in, x-xi, xiv, 47-48, 187-188
*JobShift* (Bridges), 12

Kanter, R. M., 12, 25, 88
Katzenbach, J. R., 22; *Real Change Leaders,*
  10, 79
Kelley, D., 82
Kelley, R., "How Bell Labs Creates Star
  Performers," 158-159
Kennedy, J. F., 79, 185-186
Kiechel, W., 188
Kleiner, A., *The Fifth Discipline Handbook,*
  70
knowledge economy, 203
Kotter, J., 143

lateral learning, 124; *See also* learning
Lawrence, P., 142
leadership, x; types of leaders, 27-28, 188-
  189; *See also* learning leaders
*Leadership Engine, The* (Tichy), 56
*Leadership Is an Art* (De Pree), 196
learning: and co-learning, 19-22, 56-57,
  64-65, 169; in a changing environment, 6-11, 13, 15-16, 155; defined, 7,
  10, 183; discovery, 114; feedback for,

159-162; lateral, 124; and learning his-
tories, 170-171; and life cycle of organizations, 163-167; opportunities for,
171-172; plan for, 174-178, in practice,
167-170; in shift from hierarchical to
horizontal structures, 157-159; for task
alignment, 172-174, 178-182; *See also*
learning leaders
learning leaders, 23, 203-204; as Collaborators, 47-76; competencies of, 16, 28,
29-41; defined, 3, 184; description of
role of, xii-xiv, 10-11, 14-17, 171;
as Innovators, 77-104; as Integrators,
129-152; learning to become, 157-182;
managers vs., 25-28; as Producers,
105-127; *See also* learning organizations
learning organizations: as communities of
purpose, 183-204; defined, x, 6;
from managing to mentoring in, 5-17;
mentoring relationships in, 19-28;
value of mentoring in, ix-xv; *See also*
learning leaders
*Learning to Lead* (Bennis and Goldsmith),
86
Lee, C., 197
Leslie, J. B., 162
Levinson, H., 197
life cycle of organizations, 163-167
Lipnack, J., xiv
listening, 49, 65, 189; active, 50, 52-53;
assessing skills of, 52-54; criticism of,
191-192; deep, 52, 53; *See also* communication
Lombardi, V., *Coaching for Teamwork,* 56
Lorsch, J., 142
Lowe, J., Jr., 192
loyalty ethic, xiv; in downsized organizations, x-xi, 47-48, 187-188; as part of
old psychological contracts, 20, 21,
47-48
Lynch, J., *Mentoring,* 57

Maccoby, M., 25
managerial mentors, x-xiii; defined, 183;
roles of, 30-34, 166; *See also* learning
leaders
managers, 60, 73, 107; changing psychological contracts for, 20-22, 47-48;

**214**